THE NOISE

and

The Silence

Stephen A. Braden, M.D.

The Noise and the Silence by Stephen A. Braden, M.D.
Copyright © 2020 by Stephen A. Braden
All Rights Reserved.
ISBN: 978-1-59755-661-3

Published by: ADVANTAGE BOOKS™
                  Longwood, Florida, USA
                  www.advbookstore.com

Library of Congress Catalog Number: 2021953053
RELIGION: Christian Ministry – Missions
RELIGION: Christian Life – Inspirational

First Printing: January 2022
22 23 24 25 26   10 9 8 7 6 5 4 3 2 1

Table of Contents

SECTION ONE

IF TODAY YOU HEAR HIS VOICE

Introduction

I believe that God is always trying to talk to us; we just don't listen very well. He isn't forceful, at least not most of the time; few of us ever have those "St. Paul on the road to Damascus" revelations. But He does whisper to us, wink at us, or nudge us in the most unexpected ways. I believe we just need to be willing to listen in order to hear it.

Not only is the world full of noisy colorful distractions, I often find my own mind so busy that it's hard to just be quiet inside my own head for very long. Every now and then, God succeeds in getting a word in edgewise. To me, these are powerful moments.

Over the years, I've made the mistake of thinking that such moments were private, between God and me. They are indeed very personal, but now, I feel a sense of conviction that sometimes it is good to share such stories with one another. Such messages may have relevance to others in ways I cannot know. They may even have been given to me but meant primarily for someone else. The few times I have dared to share one of these stories with someone, I have found that they themselves reacted to it as if the word (or message) was personal for them. Sometimes even opening them up to see or hear something differently than I did.

So, even though I judge myself to be a very private person, I am compelled to put these out there, and let others listen for themselves. As I think back on the times I have heard Him speak directly to me, I find more depth and meaning and application. That's one reason I believe someone else might need to hear as well.

We all have stories to tell. Some of those stories have the capacity to be real blessings for someone else. As you read, listen for yourself. What do you hear? All Christians are sent on a mission, to get to heaven and bring along as many others as possible. These stories come from lots of little missions I've experienced along the way of that one big mission. Maybe you can relate to some of the stories, even if you've never left your hometown. Where are you on your mission? Your experiences are surely different, but our sharing is part of the journey. Let Him speak to you as you read. What He tells you may be altogether your own.

Chapter 1

Can You Hear Me in the Noise? (Nueva Palestina, Honduras, 2004)

The building we were living and working in for this week was a single unit that included our sleeping quarters (bunk beds with mosquito nets, side by side), kitchen (smoky wood fireplace), dining room/pharmacy, stock room, three consultation/treatment rooms, a shower facility (of sorts), and an open courtyard complete with a water trough and roaming chickens.

One day, in the middle of the week, things got particularly crowded and noisy. Our team consisted of various health care providers, translators, and support people. The crowd of waiting patients huddled around the gated entrance; some had essentially camped out there all night.

As the day went on, our gatekeeper was in charge of letting in just enough people for us to handle at one time. Some would come in, get registered, and be asked to sit on benches in the same room where the dental team worked pulling teeth. Two chiropractors set up in another room while the other doctors and nurses set up at small tables around the open courtyard for our consultations.

The crowd outside clamored in conversation as they waited. The waiting room buzzed excitedly as they also got to watch the dentists at work. Dozens of other conversations were happening all over the rather small compound. As a team, we struggled to control the chaos in such situations. Everyone seemed to be talking at the same time. There was such a mixture of excitement, anxiety, fear, pain, relief, desperation and sometimes joy and laughter audible all day long, sometimes all at the same moment!

Personally, I have always struggled with why it has to be that way. Why such chaos? (Such a first world thought!) Why can't it be nice and quiet and calm? People could just sit quietly waiting their turn. But on this particular day I got an answer to my pondering and my internal unrest. I was stunned. I was busy, and having a hard time even hearing my own thoughts, but for one brief moment I just listened to the whole symphonic cacophony surrounding me, and then I heard a soft quiet little voice inside my head.

"Can you hear Me in the noise?"

Wait! Where did that thought come from? Was it just my imagination? It was such a simple little message, but it stopped me and made me notice a much bigger reality happening around me than I had ever realized before. This was not just a crowd of noisy people seeking medical care. It was not just a group of medical providers trying to help out a poor remote village. Those were true for sure, but God Himself was there!

He was audible to me at that moment, existing in the Noise itself. His Holy Spirit was speaking, groaning, trying to make Himself known to us. In all those people asking for our ears to listen to their needs, in all the dozens of contiguous conversations, He was present. Not "in spite of" the noise, but actually IN it. Like the "mighty rushing wind" of Pentecost, the Holy Spirit was audibly alive and flowing in that community. We had gathered in His name and He was in our midst.

I let this awareness soak in for a moment and felt a true sense of awe. As the day went on, I would occasionally just stop and listen to it all again, trying to grasp the deeper meaning of it all.

I held this in my heart until later that evening when I had the chance to share it with my wife, Michelle, asking her opinion. Was this just my own thoughts? Was my mind playing tricks on me? Or had God really spoken to me? She gave me the confidence to share this little insight with the whole group later, and several of them remarked how it rang true to them as well.

I think God speaks to us in many different ways. He wants to have as much conversation with us as we are willing to have. That conversation unfortunately is frequently one way with us pouring out our needs and concerns, but how wonderful to occasionally hear Him say something directly to us!

Surely, He speaks to us in Scripture and the Liturgy; many of us sense His presence in the wonders of nature. But on that blessed day in Nueva Palestina, I came to realize a little more clearly how He is everywhere. He is present whenever two or more of us are gathered in His name. In the desperate eyes of the poor who come to us, He is looking right at us. In our own hearts and heads, He is whispering encouragement and instructions. He is there whenever two of us connect in care, concern and love. And when a crowd of people clamors around us, He speaks out! Such a beautiful song of true community!

It is difficult to hold onto that thought. Back home, in the day-to-day routine, it is particularly hard. On mission trips I find it a little easier to focus and listen for Him. In my own office back in Texas, so often I get the feeling of being bogged down and put upon by a slightly different kind of chaos, but still a noise that I could listen to differently. Why is that? I am sure the reality is much the same. I forget about His presence and feel like I am on my own. How sad! More constant prayer throughout the day helps, and occasionally, if I take a moment to think back on that magical time in Honduras, I can barely perceive a similar message, "I'm still here, even in This noise," and I can grasp again momentarily the call to be His hands, His ears, His voice for that next person I encounter. I admit it is very hard to hold onto that. I fail a lot. But it is truly wonderful to have something like this to help me carry on with a better sense of purpose and joy!

Open your ears and listen. Can you hear Him speak to you in your daily "Noise"?

Habakkuk 3:16 says "I heard, and my inward parts trembled; at the sound my lips quivered."

The waiting crowd outside our compound.

The beautiful little village of Nueva Palestina

These two little boys and their mother live in this house made of tarps on poles.

I AM

How many ways I AM
Calling to you,
Reaching for you;
Writing, speaking, singing,
Seeking to get to you;
Words of inspiration,
Explanation, invitation.
I send angels,
Unassuming, non-demanding,
Visible and audible,
But only to the willing.

Nature's songs are myriad,
But all sing out, I AM.
Whether roaring rapids, forest glen,
Majestic mountain view,
Or simple bug on humble meadow grass,
Listen without limit to the lyrics
Of the Love that I AM.

I AM in the desperate crowd
That clamors to be near you
Seeking but a moment of your time;
A touch, a tear,
A smile, your ear...
See Me in the wrinkles
Of the elder ladies;
Feel Me in their roughened
Sacrificial hands.
Know my energy and life
In the raucous boys-
Can you hear ME in the noise?

In the bread
And in the wine,
I nurture you
To make you mine.
In communion, in confession,
In meditation
And adoration…
You turn to Me,
I run to you;
You plead to Me,
I bleed for you;
You cry to Me,
I die for you!

In life's gentle moments,
Tender touch, sweet caress;
In all the loving-kindness
Life lays upon your lap;
Know I AM,
The One who loves you!

Chapter 2

Give Her a Hug for Me!
(Tamahu, Guatemala 2011)

The St. Thomas Aquinas Catholic Church in College Station, Texas had been sending medical mission teams to Tamahu, Guatemala, for several years. Due to scheduling conflicts with another mission team, I had not been able to go along with them. Finally, in 2011 things worked out for Michelle and I to join them. As was the practice of this particular group, the local church, which served as our host, was open for us every morning for prayer, adoration and mass before dawn. We were being housed in local homes scattered around the small village, so it was up to us individually to get up and get there to participate. This practice surely helped keep us as a team, and helped keep me focused and more mindful of what we were there to do.

On this specific trip, I held in my heart a personal concern for one of my favorite Aunts back in Texas. Aunt Dorothy had been battling breast cancer for several years and had already survived many years longer than her doctors had originally predicted. It had become obvious to most of us in the family that the end was likely to be near. I even wondered if she might die while I was out of the country and I would miss the funeral.

Aunt Dorothy had been a fabulous witness throughout her illness, never losing her faith, joy and hope. Her smile was always there, in spite of her physical pain. Her concern for others outweighed her worries about herself. As I thought of her one morning in the quiet of that little chapel in Tamahu, I offered up a little prayer for her. It went something like this,

"Dear Lord, when Aunt Dorothy gets to heaven, would you please give her a big welcoming hug from me?"

What I heard in response to that prayer once again struck me in a very profound way.

"OK, I will. But for now, while she is still on this earth, I want you to give her a hug for me!"

I tried to take that in but felt overpowered, like I could not just let this thought go. It was so much more than just an idle thought passing through my head.

A few weeks later, after our return home, I had the opportunity to visit Aunt Dorothy for lunch. At the end of the meal, I felt compelled to tell her of that prayer experience in Guatemala. She listened very attentively and appreciatively. As I told her about my prayer and hearing God's message to me about her, she simply smiled and said, "I believe I could feel that prayer a few weeks ago." I did in fact then give her a hug from God.

I was blessed to visit Aunt Dorothy several times over the next few months before she passed on, and each time, I made sure to give her a hug from God, which she openly accepted. I can now sense her receiving a perfect eternal hug directly from God in heaven, and that awareness gives me such comfort.

This of course is a deeply personal story, and one I have not shared with many people. But once again, as I mull it over in my heart, I've come to realize a bigger deeper message for all of us. We often pray for others and ask God to do something for them, God hears those prayers and always knows the best way to answer them. Sometimes, He only asks of us to be His hands, His ears, His eyes, His smile, His "hugger".

What an awesome gift and responsibility!

Who might He want you to "hug for Him?"

When you pray for God to "do something", do you ever hear Him giving you the instructions on how to do it with Him?

Chapter 3

And Now You Know How I Feel! (Tamahu, Guatemala)

The Gospels are full of stories of the disciples not always getting it right. So often, Jesus had to straighten them out and even admonish them. Peter, Thomas, James and John all took turns being admonished by Jesus.

"Oh, ye of little faith!"

"Do you still not understand?"

"You do not know what you are asking…"

"Get ye behind me, Satan!"

Do we sometimes hear Him saying these words to us? Perhaps we should ponder that.

On a cool early morning back in Tamahu, we had spent our morning hour in prayer and preparation for another day on the mission. As the group came out of the church and headed down the street to our little breakfast hall my wife, Michelle, scurried ahead happily chatting with several of her friends in the group. I had come out of the church excited and wanting to stroll to breakfast together, maybe even holding hands. (Like John and Yolanda Hall always did!) I wanted to at least try to maintain some closeness to her as the day's work got underway, but seeing her run ahead left me feeling just a little miffed. It was just a thought of, "Wow! How quickly she forgot about me! She's not paying any attention to me." Just as that thought was flashing through my head, I heard, or sensed, Jesus at my right shoulder say, "Yes, I know. Now you know how I feel when you so quickly forget about Me." (Psalm 16:8)

OOPS! I, myself, had just come out of church after a wonderful intimate encounter with Christ, only to again forget that He is right beside me. How easily I was distracted by the cares of the day and my self-centeredness. It only took a few seconds for me to forget. This time I had more of a feeling of His hand touching my shoulder, stopping me in my selfish tracks, giving me my own healthy dose of humility. This thought has returned to me multiple times over the years, and I catch myself and have to ask for forgiveness yet again.

One of the prayers we focus on when on these missions is from Mother Teresa, "let us serve Christ in His distressing disguise of the poor." We try to stay focused on this for one special week, but I am acutely (and sometimes painfully) aware of how much harder it is to maintain that focus back home in the mundane day to day. Are my patients back here in Texas not just as much 'Christ in disguise'? Are not my family, friends and coworkers?

Lord, have mercy on me. Help me recognize and serve You in the distressing disguise of the whiney, demanding, neurotic, sad, tired folk who come to see me every day at my office! When I am judgmental, critical, and irritated, speak to me again. When things don't go my way, help me surrender and listen to your gentle guiding voice.

NITTY-GRITTY LOVE

Love isn't always pretty,
It isn't always fine.
But it's in the nitty-gritty
That love truly is divine.

If everything were easy
And the way was always smooth,
We'd have no need to listen
To the whisperings of truth.

The fact is we all struggle.
We stumble and we fall.
But in finding grace to stand again
We heed our saintly call.

So, amid the daily chaos
As you strive to rise above,
Know you are a sign to others
Of what it means to love.

Chapter 4

The Theology of Tears
(Driving down Texas roads)

The ways the Spirit speaks to us go far beyond words, and some thoughts and feelings are hard to articulate. I recalled an article in *The Catholic Spirit*, our diocesan newspaper from June 2016 by Cindy Wooten about Pope Francis and his "theology of tears." That article rang very true to me.

Pope Francis wrote how tears are sometimes a more eloquent means of communication than our attempts with words. My wife and I have shed many genuine tears through our journey together: the loss of a pregnancy, the struggles of raising our children, dealing with obstacles on our travels to remote corners of this world to name a few. Tears have been an expression of sadness, fear, pain, but also of compassion and joy.

Tears have often factored into my discernment process when trying to decide whether or not some thought of mine is spiritually valid and/or worthy of being written down. As I ponder such questions the tears often well up and announce a sense of goodness and confirmation. When I re-read something later, and the tears return, I am even more assured. If someone else reads one of these reflections and I see the tears in their eyes as well, then I know even more certainly that I have heard correctly. Tears serve as a tangible, physical connection between our minds, souls, and bodies.

I am something of a bird watcher. Another way Christ frequently gets my attention and offers encouragement and consolation is by having a beautiful bird (particularly hawks) just happening to appear at the precise moment I need it. I make a habit of watching for hawks as I drive the Texas highways, but sometimes they appear as more of a sign, like an angel, or the Holy Spirit. (Like doves appear so often in Scripture.)

One example of a time when both of these means of consolation hit me with a sort of double-whammy was on a drive from Bryan to Round Rock for a meeting with the Austin Medical Mission Board. I had been quietly driving and recalled a story from my youth about my grandfather. "PawPaw" and I had gone out to the back porch to shuck some fresh corn for dinner that evening. As we went about this task, he paused for a moment and held up one of the ears of corn. He looked at it with a sense of simple awe and remarked how this ear of corn spoke to him of God's miraculous creation. Such a wonderful design, a thing of beauty! Only God could make something so marvelous. He didn't say much more, but he encouraged me, as a young boy, to try and be aware of the beauty of creation that surrounds us every day and give God the credit for all of it. He was a quiet man, much like myself, but that moment when he shared his soul's awe toward God has stuck with me my whole life.

So, would this little story be worth writing down to share later with my own grandchildren or even other folks?

As that question passed through my mind, I felt the tears begin to well. I sensed that oh so familiar warmth within my heart. But that could just be my nostalgic emotions, right? Christ was not through, just a few seconds later I spotted a beautiful red hawk posing in a tree beside the road. Wham! But even that was not all. Only seconds later a companion hawk could be seen sitting on a branch just up the road. Wham, wham!

This whole process occurred in less than a minute, but I had the soul-deep awareness of the authenticity of the value of sharing such a simple testimony. It even now makes me think of how I am being watched by my kids, grandkids, friends etc. They may be taking notes of what I say and do even when I don't know it. My opportunities to make positive impacts are there and I should be mindful of that.

I also recall the gift of tears as I struggled to write my mother's eulogy. It was like the tears were washing my eyes and helping me see more clearly, trying to compose something worthy of her. The tears flowed so freely that whole night. It was the first time I felt I could pray to this new saint in heaven. The consolation of those tears let me know I was not alone.

I'll come back to tears again later.

Luke 7: 37-38, 50 says, "Now there was a sinful woman in the city who learned that he was at table in the house of the Pharisee. Bringing an alabaster flask of ointment, she stood behind him at his feet weeping and began to bathe his feet with her tears. Then she wiped them with her hair, kissed them, and anointed them with the ointment. He said to the woman, 'your faith has saved you; go in peace.'"

How has God sent His consolations to you?

In what special little ways has He spoken to you?

If you have never felt or heard God's voice in any personal way, ask Him. Then make an effort to pay more attention. We hear more when we listen. We see more when we are watching!

Stephen A Braden, M.D.

Chapter 5

I Am Here
(Maggoty, Jamaica)

As a Catholic, Confession or Reconciliation is a wonderful opportunity to hear God speak to us yet again. During such a time in our parish, I confessed to the priest some of my struggles with wanting to be in charge and how often I get critical and short with others when I don't get my way. I lose my focus on my calling to be a joyful caring compassionate minister and instead act as a snarling bossy old goat. Some at my office have nicknamed me 'Grumpy'. This frequent occurrence troubles me and I felt the need to mention it to the priest. He skillfully pointed out the underlying pride that makes me want to be in charge of everything- when the reality is that I have no control over anything in life except my own free will.

God alone is God, and He is in charge of everything about the schedule of my life. I do not even have the guarantee that I will live to see the end of the day! At the end of our discussion, the priest gave me a simple penance: to say a simple prayer as I start my day at work, and then whenever necessary during the day. This prayer is, "Lord, I am here," just that, nothing more. I have practiced this since and usually my mind wants to add more verbiage, but keeping it simple is important. Sometimes the simplicity escapes me, but if I stick to it, it works.

I recognize that most of my prayers are me trying to make a nice speech to God, but it should be more conversational; talk/ listen, talk/listen, listen some more!

Sometime later, on a subsequent trip to Jamaica, I was volunteering in a small clinic, which had been built on the site of Holy Spirit Catholic Church in Maggoty. Once again, the days were structured such that mornings began with prayer in the chapel with just the priest, nuns and a few locals in attendance. As I sat there one morning and tried to psych myself up for the coming day in clinic, I recalled that need for this little prayer exercise. In the quiet room, surrounded by those half dozen others,

I said that little phrase, "Lord, I am here," and then I sensed Him again, in response to me He said, "I AM here."

The great I AM is here! Just like He had made Himself present to me back in Honduras when He asked me to hear Him in the Noise, He now asked me to continue to know His presence and bask in it. I am not alone, no matter how I feel. EVER! Whenever I acknowledge to Him that I am here, wherever that is and whatever I am doing, the great I AM is there with me. This simple prayer is designed to make me more aware of that marvelous fact.

He had confirmed to me the truth of Matthew 18: 20, "For where two or more have gathered in My name, there I am in their midst."

Later in the day, as I worked in the clinic, I found myself needing to repeat this prayer, and this time, with a twinkle of joy, I heard His response again, and again. His voice sounded happy and smiling like that famous portrait of the "Smiling Jesus".

I hope that all who read this will try this simple prayer for themselves, and even more importantly, listen for His loving response to you!

Not in Charge

I am not in charge,
I AM is.
I am not the boss,
But I am loved
By the One Who IS!
I am His.

Chapter 6

Butterfly, Flutter By...
(Maggoty, Jamaica)

I have known for some years now that going to a foreign country to work on a medical mission for a week or so is as much about my own need for a retreat as it is about the health care needs of those I will see there. Almost everyone who has been on such a trip will remark about getting so much more out of the experience than we put into it ourselves. It has also become clear to me, over time, that even though we do our best to provide what we can for the medical needs we encounter, the more important aspect of each trip is the sense of the Church doing what it is supposed to be doing: reaching out to those in need, inviting the lost and lonely into the Kingdom, sharing our personal stories and our riches, expanding our vision, and encountering God in a new way.

Many of these trips have been full of humbling surprises that teach me to know my place and avoid the trap of seeing myself in some other light than that which is truly mine by the grace of God. The places we have returned to several times have more clearly brought out the need for building relationship and community rather than simply donating material goods. Those things we bring are surely appreciated by those who would not otherwise have them, but the opportunity to experience a sense of communion with someone we would not otherwise know is, in my opinion, a more valuable treasure.

In the summer of 2017, Michelle, and I made plans to return to work at the Holy Spirit Clinic in Maggoty, Jamaica. My sister, Celeste, (a dentist) was joining us. Our initial plan was to be there during the absence of their usual doctor, my friend Jeff. He would be back home in Texas at that time, so it seemed to us like a good time to go and help at the clinic.

But then came the hurricane season of 2017!

Hurricane Harvey hit Texas the last week of August and drenched the gulf coast for several days, leaving the city of Houston, and its airports, flooded and out of commission. We were scheduled to fly out on September 9th, so we waited and prayed hoping the airports might be operational in time. Two days before our flight the airport re-opened its international service, and our flight was declared a go.

We drove to Houston that morning, passing through neighborhoods wrecked by the flooding. What a sobering sight! Eventually, we made it to the airport and all the way to our gate, checked in and ready. And we waited, and waited. Then we got the news that the next hurricane, Irma, was crossing the Caribbean and wreaking its own havoc there. Although Jamaica was spared direct damage, all radar over the area had been knocked out by the storm. Unfortunately, no flights would be able to come or go through the region until the radar could be fixed, so we had no choice but to cancel our plans and drive home.

Our plan B developed over the next few days. I decided to change my trip dates to be there the first week of October. Michelle would not be able to go then, but my sister could. And, as a bonus to me, my friend Jeff would be there as well!

On the downside, our friends, Sister Emila and Father Mark would not be there as they would be on a trip back to Emila's previous stomping grounds in Bolivia. Although this did enter into my considerations, I can say that the overall drive to go was more related to a desire to simply be there and do whatever I would be called to do each day. I resigned myself to simply try and accept that reality and just let it be what it would be.

The week turned out to be one of the best retreat experiences I have ever had. Our arrival at the airport fell within an hour of another small group of visitors coming from Chicago, so picking us up at the airport was considerably more convenient for our hosts, who had to drive two hours from Maggotty to get to the airport.

I had considered my previous experiences on mission trips and my own need to stay focused. I wanted some help to avoid the traps of self-centeredness and I prayerfully asked for some inspiration for this particular trip. I was still looking for that inspiration when, on the first day on the island, the heat reminded me of how I had previously missed good old Texas air conditioning, and how I had come to appreciate every little breeze that would occasionally waft through the clinic bringing a palpable feeling of 'Aahh'. When I felt one such breeze it was like the Holy Spirit had just blown me a kiss and said, "Peace be with you!"

This became my prayer for the week. Every time I would feel a gentle breeze, I would take it as a whisper from Him, just a touch, calling me back from my mental meanderings. And it worked.

But that's not all. He also caught my eye out the back window of my exam room every now and then when a little butterfly would just quietly flutter by. As I saw the butterflies, I tried to appreciate their simple small miraculous beauty, I heard the first line of a new poem form in my head: "Butterfly, flutter by, Holy Spirit saying, 'Hi'."

So now I had two simple ways to 'touch base' in prayer throughout the day, reminding me that I am never alone. He wants so much for us to be aware of His presence. I had just asked for one simple way to do that but was abundantly blessed with two very effective answers.

Having thus proactively (intentionally) started the week, other blessings became a daily occurrence. We had been told initially that since Father Mark would not be there, we could not have daily mass. Bummer. But Jeff and the nuns came up with an alternate plan; we would start each day with a short drive to Balaclava about 15 minutes away. There was a group of "Missionaries of Charity" nuns there who ran a nursing home and had a small chapel where they also had early morning mass every day. We could make it there and back in time for a quick breakfast before our start of clinic. One problem solved! (Not to mention how many butterflies were to be seen on this drive every day!)

And the week held even more surprises. October 4th is the feast of St. Francis of Assisi. Both Jeff and Celeste are "secular Franciscans," and they spoke of their desire to attend what is called a "Transitus" service on the eve of his feast day. This is a tradition of the Franciscan order I had never heard about. Unfortunately, the nearest such service would be held nearly an hour away and started in the late afternoon. We usually did not finish the clinic service that early, so they had resigned themselves to simply doing their own service in our little house that evening. However, because we were both working, and the clinic was not double booked, we actually finished our workday quite early. So, we hopped in the car and off we went to St. Agnes Church in Chester Castle to attend the service there. (Again, butterflies fluttering by all along the way!)

Not only did we arrive early but the priest in charge asked if one of us could do one of the scripture readings. Jeff and Celeste both volunteered me and how could I refuse? Actually, it was a tremendous honor. This service was a tribute to the passage of St. Francis from this world to the next. There was a wonderful feeling of sanctity and reverence, which hit me in a profound way. This service should be required training for anyone involved with hospice ministry!

The more personal surprise blessing mixed in for Celeste and I was the fact that October 6th would mark the one-year anniversary of our brother David's very similar passing into sainthood. Such a soothing reminder to us of the reality of our heavenly hopes which so overshadows our carnal distaste of death.

Our other evenings were spent either in quiet restful reading and reflection, or friendly conversations with the small community that is the Holy Spirit parish. Friday morning, we spent our work time making house calls on a group of homebound elderly folk. We replenished their prescriptions and brought some food and other necessary supplies. Again, though, it was the time spent just visiting with them that meant the most. Several of these people are very close to their own "transitus", and we made a point of talking about that and trying to share our vision of that "heavenly hope".

The following day, Celeste and I returned to Texas. I left feeling refreshed, comforted, restored, amazed, encouraged and inspired. Not all mission trips are this reflective and prayerful and peaceful. Many are full of grueling hard work that seriously try my fiber and tax my patience. These provide much opportunity to learn and grow. I'm very grateful for this experience, and every gentle breeze that caressed my face and all the dancing butterflies that did their part to keep me tuned in to God's presence. And by the way, Texas is full of both butterflies and gentle breezes!

JAMAICAN RETREAT

Day to day drudgery
Distractions and worry,
Schedules and numbers,
Temptation to hurry.

"Pray without ceasing!"
Not words, but a Being.
Stripped down to essence-
Awareness of Presence.

Butterfly fluttering by-
Holy Spirit saying "Hi!"

The Noise and the Silence

The touch of a breeze,
A whisper of "Peace!"
"Squeaking swing-set" symphony
Of tiny Jamaican frogs;
Another fine example of
"All Creatures Great and Small"
Exotic moonrise over palm trees
Begins her joyful dance of praise
Across the stage of heaven.

In love with Love;
Let others see!
"Abide in Me!"
Be with me! Now IS eternity

Chapter 7

More of Butterflies and Breezes (Teleman, Guatemala, 2020)

In March 2020, our mission trip took us to yet another new location. The previous parishes in the state of Alta Vera Paz, Guatemala (Tamahu and San Cristobal) that had hosted our group for the previous dozen or so years had changed leadership and the new priests were not as enthusiastic for us to come for a visit. So, rather than cancel altogether, the local people who really wanted us made inquiries down the road a bit at Teleman. Their pastor was quite excited at being given this opportunity, so plans were made for us to travel there instead.

This was a new, smaller, location, poorer, and at least an hour further down the road. Because of this, we were not sure of many of the details. The decision was made to take a smaller group, just 20 instead of our usual 40. This turned out to be a mixed blessing. Logistically it was much easier to keep the smaller group on the same page. Our gracious hosts were not as overwhelmed by us and they were able to accommodate us quite comfortably. At least most of us had rooms with running water and even showers. (Sorry, Ralph!)

Our transportation from the little village of Teleman to the even tinier rural settings where we would work was the typical old yellow school bus. We crossed swollen rivers but at least we did not have to wade across them like we did in the southern part of Guatemala the preceding October rainy season. The crowds we encountered were substantial but not overwhelming for our small team.

On our third such excursion, we arrived in the little compound and unloaded. As per routine, we scoped out the facilities and tried to determine who should work in which space. This day we used both the small chapel (for registration, Physical therapy, and clothing supplies) while the dentists, doctors and pharmacy would hold court in the adjacent building, which I would suppose was an activity center of sorts. While setting up that morning, I kept noticing the abundance of prayer prompting butterflies frolicking about the grounds, a good start for the day.

By mid-afternoon, the heat started to build up in our crowded little office. That's when I noticed a slightly stronger breeze gently blow through to cool us just a bit. ("The touch of a breeze.") I took note and smiled to myself and the thought crossed my head that I could not look outside (no windows, and the doors pretty well blocked by curious onlookers) to see if the butterflies were still fluttering about.

That's when He nudged me, "Look right in front of you."

What? There was a family of five people sitting in front of me in the middle of our crowded room. What do you mean?

Again, "Look right in front of you."

I don't understand.

I just kept going with my exam of the seven year-old girl sitting before me, and then I saw it. As I started to place my stethoscope on her chest to listen to her heart, I noticed a big beautiful butterfly picture on her shirt.

"See!"

I had to stop for a second and let the smile explode on my face. It wasn't just the picture of a butterfly on her shirt; it was His presence in this beautiful little girl sitting right in front of me. (Think Mark 9:37 or Matthew 18:5). I had almost let it slip by unnoticed. Once again, He had surprised me with a gift that I almost missed out on. I wonder now how many others I did let slip by. Although I am sorry for those missed chances to feel His presence, I am so grateful for the way He persistently tries to get my attention.

Tap, tap, "Hey, psst!"

"Butterfly, fluttering by,
 Holy Spirit saying 'Hi!'
The touch of a breeze, a whisper of 'Peace.' "
LOOK RIGHT IN FRONT OF YOU!
Amen.

Has God ever just surprised you with some unexpected gift?

Do you feel tempted to blow those off as a simple coincidence?

We see more when we are watching. We hear more when we listen.

How might you be more intentional to watching and listening in your everyday life?

Section 2

Harden Not Your Heart

I have to admit that sometimes I catch myself resisting the prompting voice of the Spirit, and it is blatant and painful on my part. Other times, it is more subconscious and a simple decision to just ignore what He is saying. That may be for various reasons, like my concern for my own comfort and reputation, but I do not want God to say of me what He did about the grumbling children of Israel at Meribah and Massah! (Psalms 95)

God asks of me to carry on in the mission He has for me; my task is to be obedient. But that is far from easy sometimes. Some lessons learned along the way need reinforcing and repetition. My stubbornness is the issue. I make an effort to be intentional, but I pray for His continued patience in making me into the best version of myself. Matthew Kelly, in many of his books, encourages us to make "holy moments". This is just a matter of our decision to be aware of Him in the present moment, wherever that is. When we open our hearts to Him, He joyfully comes in as deeply as we will let Him. These next few stories relate a little of my own struggles to listen and obey. I'd ask you to reflect for yourself as you read and see if you can relate. How open are you to His loving nudges?

Stephen A Braden, M.D.

Chapter 8

Wash Her Feet (Tamasopo, Mexico)

My dear friend, Dr. Rick Barrett, a chiropractor from Sugarland, Texas, had joined our medical mission group from Austin on several of our trips to Arteaga, Mexico. His home parish had a similar mission group that annually traveled to Tamasopo, Mexico. He had invited me to come along with them on multiple occasions, so, finally one year I decided to take him up on his offer. Their team was considerably larger than those I was used to, fifty plus people, which led to some interesting logistics. One of the differences was that each day we were broken into smaller groups to travel out to tiny outlying locations to serve those who lived in truly rural settings.

On one such day, I got into the van with about ten others and we drove to a small farmhouse past thousands of acres of sugar cane. It felt like we were miles from any named village. The small group that surrounded the house welcomed us on our arrival and helped us set up our little clinic for the day. Our one dentist would use the kitchen because the light was better, and water was more available. I and the one other M.D. were each assigned a room for our use. The team of oculists would work outside under a shade tree because they needed the light to better test vision and prescribe glasses. We set up our meager equipment and went about our routine of consultations and examinations.

I was pretty much by myself in my little room most of the day. I could walk out to the pharmacy when I needed to, and then escort my next patient into my consultation room. I could look out the one window of my room and watch the eye team doing their work. At times I felt slightly jealous of their fresh air setting. My room was adequate, but dimly lit, by the single window. I frequently had to use my flashlight to examine my patients more closely.

When one such patient mentioned a problem with her feet, I tried to get a better look at them. Removing her simple sandals and shining my flashlight only revealed feet caked with dirt that completely obscured the skin I needed to see. I was suspicious that she might have an underlying "athlete's foot" fungus infection, and I was initially tempted (I use that word precisely!) to just tell her to go home, wash her feet, and then apply a prescribed anti-fungal cream until her symptoms were resolved.

But then a soft urging little whisper spoke to me and countered that temptation, "Wash her feet."

I paused and let the conversation quietly play out inside my head.

"You don't have time to do that. Other people are waiting."

"Wash her feet."

"That would just be awkward. She'll think you're weird."

"Wash her feet."

"Her feet will just get dirty again when she walks home!"

"Wash her feet."

Finally, I looked her in the eyes and told her to wait a minute. I went into the kitchen where the dentist was working. There I found a small basin and asked to borrow a towel. I returned to my exam room and told her I wanted to wash her feet so I could show her how to apply the medicated cream more precisely. In silence, I proceeded to do so. I poured a little water over her feet and gently scrubbed off the layer of dirt. I knelt before her, feeling a sense of humble servitude. I did not speak, and even my thoughts seemed to go quiet, I just did my task and let my hands speak to her. She too was quiet as she watched and allowed me to serve her in this way.

Once I had her feet as clean as I could get them, I used my flashlight to examine them once again. This confirmed my initial suspicion. I applied the first dose of her cream and explained that she would need to do this routine at home at least once a day for the next week. I felt better that my hands-on demonstration would be more likely to bring about a successful result than just telling her how to do it. I also gave her some soap to use at home.

When we were finished with the visit, we stood and simply hugged for a moment giving each other another blessing as we parted ways. No one else witnessed with this lady, and I did not share this with anyone until some time later. I don't know exactly what that sweet lady thought of me, but I suspected, as we parted, that she had been as blessed as I had been. Her appreciation and gratitude felt genuine. My soul felt humbled, fresh and light.

The layers of meaning and lessons to be learned by this experience have continued for me over the years. I have watched many others provide similar service since that time, whether for clinical need like wound care, or to simply be better able to fit the person with a new pair of shoes and socks.

Lovingly washing someone's feet is so much more than a "symbol" or a ritual to be re-enacted once a year on Holy Thursday. In Matthew 25, Jesus says, "Amen, I say to you, whatever you did for one of these least brothers of mine, you did for me." (Matt. 25:40). He does NOT say, "it was almost like you were doing it to Me."

It helps me on a regular basis to revisit such experiences. Jesus doesn't just cross our paths once in a great while; He meets us daily numerous times. My own ability to keep that in mind is weak and faulty. That fact bothers me often, but I am trying to learn to accept my weakness and just rejoice when I do succeed in recognizing Him!

Sometimes I hear His Spirit nudging me to reach out to some struggling soul in need of His touch. Submitting to such nudging can be uncomfortable, but I must continue to try. Sometimes the fruit of such an encounter is readily available to be enjoyed. Other times I am left hoping that some seed has been planted for someone else to harvest at a later date. Our "success" doesn't matter, our "faithfulness" does (St. Theresa of Calcutta).

Letting the love of the Spirit flow through us and letting Him minister to us at the same moment, can feel miraculous. Such miracles can and do happen in our daily lives, even back home in Texas. I am forever grateful for having encountered Him in that little farmhouse in "God Knows Where", Mexico.

John 13: 1-15 (The washing of the feet)

Matthew 25: 31-46 (Whatsoever you did…)

How does Jesus ask you to "wash the feet" of others?

Do you sometimes try to "rationalize" or talk yourself out of the invitations of the Holy Spirit?

Are there certain people who challenge you to "see Christ in His distressing disguise?"

So many opportunities to be the loving hands of Jesus.

Stephen A Braden, M.D.

Chapter 9

Who Are You Really Coming to See? (Tamahu, Guatemala)

One of the more challenging but fun times on some of our trips is when we get to go on a hike to reach even more remote villages that have no usable roads. Having done that on several occasions in the past, I was looking forward to the possibility as we returned for another visit to Tamahu, Guatemala.

The town of Tamahu is modest in size but reaching out to their suburbs, where the indigenous people still speak mostly Mayan dialects, is even a more of a challenge. Some of these people rarely, if ever, make the trip into town themselves. Having to tote our supplies with us is another obstacle, but that is all part of the fun!

On this particular trip, we were initially told that we would not have any hiking excursions, which was a bummer. So, when the local priest relented and told us that some of us could make a quick half-day trip up the hill to a small village, I was glad to go. We would be limited in time, leaving late morning. We'd have to hike a couple miles up a hill, set up, see the locals, and get down before the late afternoon rains would hit. About a dozen or so of us hardier souls were chosen for this trek, while the remainder would continue their work in Tamahu.

We managed the hike up with no real calamity, just a long uphill hike. I'll admit I had to stop and rest a couple of times going up. Along with me were a couple of nurses, some translators, Michelle (pharmacist and supply organizer extraordinaire), several college students in various stages of career discernment, and our Sherpas (local men who were capable of carrying heavy duffle-bags full of supplies).

We arrived to find a tiny village on the side of the mountain, from which we could look down to see Tamahu. We set up our makeshift clinic on the front porch of the small school building, which unfortunately was locked. We registered the folks at one end of the porch, sat them down on benches, did our interviews and exams, made our assessments and handed out the medications and supplies as best we could, and as fast as we could.

As the line was finally getting to the end, and I knew we were about out of time, I felt a tap on my shoulder. One of the translators told me that I was needed to make a house call on a man who was having some kind of back problem and could not come to us. His daughter had been sent to fetch me to his house. To be honest, my first reaction was one of being just a little put out.

"I don't have time for this!", I thought. I did not know what he might need; I did not know how far away this house might be. I turned to Michelle and told her of this request to ask her advice. She matter-of-factly told me, "Maybe this is the one person we came up here to see."

With that perspective, I told the two nurses to carry on with the remaining few folks on our porch. I grabbed my little black bag and headed down the narrow trail with my translator and the little girl. I said a quick prayer for help and guidance as we trudged along the muddy path, through banana orchards and coffee bushes, and as we made the last turn, the little girl indicated that this was the place. We entered a fenced-in dirt yard and I saw the little shack of a house so typical of this region.

At the front of the house was a worktable and bench with several pieces of lumber leaning against it. There was a pile of wood shavings and sawdust on the ground by the table. The picture in front of me struck me as a scene one might see on a Christmas card where Jesus is working alongside St. Joseph in Nazareth at the carpenter shop.

At that moment, and I do mean that exact moment, I heard that little Voice yet again whisper in my ear, "Can I make it any more clear to you Who you are really coming to see!"

And again, I was stunned and awed. I felt humbled as I entered the house and saw the waiting family. I was introduced and shown to the bed wherein lay my patient. His name was Don Pedro, and he was sort of the mayor of this village of San Pedro. He had been sick for several weeks, and a few weeks earlier he had gone down to Tamahu with back pain, fever, and he was urinating blood. The doctor there had given him an antibiotic injection and sent him home. The blood had cleared up, but he still had some back pain and occasional fever and was very weak.

I did the best I could to assess the medical issues and decide on a treatment plan, and then I excused myself and literally ran back to our little clinic on the school porch. I asked Michelle to get some of our injectable antibiotics ready, some follow up oral medications, and a bag of supplies for the family. Luckily, we had a couple gallons of pure water left which we used to dissolve several packets of rehydration material. As quick as I could get it all gathered, I ran back to Don Pedro's house and gave him the shot, explained all the other medications and supplies to the family, said a quick prayer for them and said my good-byes. They were extremely gracious and warm people, the "Holy Family," and I could not get over the humbling feeling of being blessed to be there.

Again, I returned to our group at the school, and we packed up what little we had left and headed back down the mountain. I felt overwhelmed and elated, and I actually burst out singing "Climb Every Mountain" at one point. About halfway down the hill the rains came. We donned our ponchos and kept going, slipping and sloshing happily as darkness began to fall. Eventually we did make it back into town. The roads were full of water and all electricity was out in town due to the storm, but we marched joyfully into the churchyard to a wonderful reception from our prayerful companions.

I tried to share some of this story with our group, but I never knew if I was adequately able to express how powerful these experiences are. We are all called to go beyond ourselves in whatever situation the Lord leads us. Some of these are true "mountain top experiences" like in San Pedro, but more often He asks us to serve Him in our mundane day to day situations. But, I have to admit having such mountain top experiences in my memory bank surely helps. I hope I have not failed totally in recognizing Him in those who cross my daily paths. I know I do sometimes, but I remind myself to open my eyes and try to keep in mind, "Who are you really coming to see!"

Psalm 43: 3 Send your light and your fidelity, that they may be my guide, let them bring me to your holy mountain to the place of your dwelling.

Here's another little poem I wrote after a different hike in Alta Vera Paz, Guatemala, that expresses some similar feelings. Seeing a wood worker and his sawdust piles along our rain muddied trail reminded me of my meeting with Don Pedro, while the crowd of humble people we ministered to in the small chapel that day reminded me once again to be aware of His presence.

Alta Vera Paz

Step by step,
Slosh and squish,
Slip and slide,

Stephen A Braden, M.D.

Climbing, falling, rising up...
Chainsaw, axe whacks...
Sawdust paths.

Silence, glances,
Smiles and stares...
Expectations, fears...
Glares.

Fidgets and squeaks,
Squeals and sniffles...
Chirps and whistles,
Laughter, giggles,
Weeping.

Every one,
One more note
In the symphony of our days...
Our offering of praise.

Chapter 10

I'm Out of Gas
(Guanagazapa, Esquintla, Guatemala)

In October 2014, we had the opportunity to return to a small town in Guatemala for our third visit there. Guanagazapa is a delightful little town that had welcomed us before and was glad for our return. The people in charge of this visit had arranged for us to use a civic auditorium/gym for our clinic instead of the smaller facility behind the church we had used before. We were a much larger group of providers this time around, and the waiting crowd was exponentially larger as well.

Toward the end of the afternoon it got quite warm in the building and my energy was running very low. We had seen several hundred people and the decision had been made to stop putting more people into the triage area. As my line of waiting patients finally came to an end, I took a deep breath and declared to myself, "I'm done for the day!"

Unbeknownst to me, some of the others on the team had decided to go into the parking garage below us and try to see to the needs of a couple hundred more people. They were just passing out vitamins and pain medications and clothing, but a surprise was in store for us all.

The very last person in that group was a young mother with a son who apparently was somewhat ill. She could only get the attention of one of the security guards who was helping just to control the crowd. She showed him the boy's stomach and he immediately got the attention of one of the nurses, who grabbed the P.A., who grabbed Dr. Rudy, who said, "Take this boy up to Steve!" Liz brought him up to me where I was about to put away all my instruments and get ready to relax.

Liz announced to me, with her usual smile, that I had one more patient to see. My first response was, "No, I'm done," but she insisted that I needed to look at him. I again told her, "No, I'm out of gas. There is no way." But she persisted one last time and just told me to look at his stomach. So, I did.

My heart sunk, and I sighed. He was an eight or nine year-old boy who looked mildly ill, but when we lifted up his shirt, I saw a rather large sore. It looked red and felt warm. I would estimate it to have been about ten cm. in size, raised and fluctuant. He also had a lot of other smaller sores, typical of impetigo. My judgment was that one of those had developed into a full-blown abscess. The boy needed this abscess taken care of, and I was the one with the minor surgery kit. It was my job to take care of him. I did not want to accept that. Surely there was another answer?

But no, it was up to me. So, I told Liz to get me some help. I would get the surgical supplies ready, but I needed one of the nurses to help me. As the dentist group had finished for the day, I elected to use one of their nice reclining chairs for my operation. Dr. Celeste, one of the dentists, let me use some of their needles and syringes for the anesthesia injection. They also had plenty of necessary gloves and drapes we could use. We had to explain the situation and necessary procedure to the boy's mother and get her verbal consent to the draining of the abscess. A couple nurses also came over to help. Translators were constantly giving reassurance to the boy and his family. I had to give him an injection of anesthetic and then I could proceed to make an incision into the abscess. As I leaned over him to work, the sweat on my face made my glasses slip down my nose. Dr. Rick, the chiropractor, graciously wiped my brow and then literally held my glasses in place while I worked. Eduardo, the nurse helped, me to actually drain as much of the pus as we could get out. As we irrigated the wound and applied even more pressure to the area trying to get all the pus out, the boy started crying and needed the other two nurses to help calm him and keep him still.

Finally, as we finished and got him bandaged up, I asked them to give him a couple more injections: one for pain and one with an antibiotic. I moved on to arranging for follow up care with Cora, one of our local friends and one of the organizers. She helped me get an understanding of the local resources. There was no hospital or even a good local health clinic available in Guanagazapa, and I wanted him seen the next day to be sure he was okay, but we were not going to be anywhere nearby ourselves. The nearest hospital was in the town down the road, Esquintla, but he would have to be transported there (one problem) and would have to be able to pay something just to get seen at the hospital (another problem). I got an estimate from her for the cost of those matters and just took out my wallet and gave her enough to see to the arrangements. It wasn't all that much money, but it was more than the family would have.

As other medications were supplied to the family and all explanations were finalized, I began trying to take stock of this whole event. One of my first thoughts was, "Why does God always seem to save these types of cases until the end of the day, when I am nearly exhausted?"

Again, I think God has both a wonderful sense of humor and the amazing knack for making us more acutely aware that He is in charge, not us. I am not supposed to be doing great things on my own. He just wants me to be constantly in His presence, depending on Him and His power to accomplish whatever needs to be done. He wants me to see my dependence on the whole Body of Christ of which I am just one part. I have the option to say "No", whenever I choose. But He keeps inviting me to be part of His greater plan. That plan is always so much greater than I can fathom.

Over the next few days, I got updates from Cora, who was able to reassure me that the boy was seen at the hospital and that all had turned out well for him. The family was very grateful, and the local community was impressed. I grew more aware of the beauty of the Body of Christ and how we function in concert even sometimes when we don't see the big picture. Each of us has specific gifts, which may be inadequate if left alone, but work very nicely when blended with those of our brothers and sisters. I heard one description of this in a beautiful reflection recently, how we are "jig-sawed together." I also love the image of us as individual threads divinely woven into a heavenly tapestry.

The mother of the young boy had the gift of loving determination to get her son seen. The security guard had the gumption to step out of his role of crowd control and get the boy seen by a nurse. The nurse had the wisdom to speed the triage process. Liz had the compassion to spend her last energy down in that hot garage passing out items to those poor people, putting her in line to get this boy seen in the first place. The nurses lent their expertise to his medical needs. Dr. Celeste and Dr. Rick helped keep me calm and focused (literally!). Cora offered her organizational skills and knowledge of the local situation to get the follow up arranged. The list of all who contributed goes on and on, and I am sure that there are many parts to this story I will never be fully aware of. I am even now mindful of how many people were supporting us in prayer back home, and how many had also contributed financially to make this whole endeavor possible. I know that many folks were touched in some way, and that this will have an impact on their spiritual beings. Hopefully this will then lead them to be a little more likely to pay it forward someday. Maybe even I will be more ready to respond to the daily opportunities to serve others graciously in the name of Jesus who sends me forth, maybe. Amen!

1 Corinthians 12:4-6 "There are different kinds of spiritual gifts but the same Spirit; there are different forms of service by the same Lord; there are different workings but the same God who produces all of them in everyone."

When you are asked to do some less than desirable task, can you try to see it as part of God's providential plan?

How easy/hard is it for you to submit and be a "gracious giver?"

Can you see yourself as a vital part of the Body of Christ?

If you decide not to do your part, will it just not get done?

Chapter 11

One Last House Call
(Maggoty Pass, Jamaica)

In August of 2014, Michelle and I were privileged to make our first trip to Maggoty, Jamaica and the local Catholic Church staffed by Father Mark Z, and several nuns, missionaries from Poland. This Holy Spirit Church had also established a lovely little clinic to help tend to the medical needs of the poor inhabitants of Maggoty and the surrounding communities, and volunteer medical personnel had come from both Europe and North America to help in their efforts. My good friend Dr. Jeff K. had discovered this gold mine of ministry and invited us to participate.

As I have shared already, the days here begin with morning prayers as a group, holy mass, and then breakfast. The clinic is open from 8-5 Monday through Thursday with Friday reserved for making house calls. We could expect to see somewhere between fifty and ninety patients per day. Some by appointment, but others simply show up and get in line. Most patients even had charts to review, and needed chronic medications refilled. Some needed food and other supplies as well. The devoted nuns did the best they could to accommodate them. Temperatures there are always warm, sometimes flat out hot, and cold showers at the end of each day provide a refreshing respite.

Sister Emila was our guide on the house calls. She would prepare a bag of medications and supplies for each patient to be seen along with their charts. On the very last day of our work, she mentioned that there was still one more patient to be seen late that afternoon that we had not been able to get to that morning. We loaded back into the car with her and Stanley, our chauffeur, drove us just a mile or two up the hill to Maggoty Pass, a suburb of Maggoty. This village was much like many of the poorer areas we had visited in Central America. No real clean water supply, just a pipe with a hose, from which everyone got buckets of water to carry to their houses.

We did the expected house call on an elderly lady with hypertension and arthritis, and as we finished, I breathed a little sigh of relief as I thought we were through for the week. That's when Sister Emila announced that there was, in fact, yet one more patient to be seen. She herself, however, had to get back to the convent to cook supper for our celebration dinner that evening. So, she handed us over to a local gentleman who would show us where to go. She gave me the last supply bag and she was off with Stanley in the car while we dutifully followed our guide up a path to a small concrete blockhouse at the top of the hill.

This was a simple two-room building where our guide's mother lived. His daughter met us at the door. She was a very nice young lady who was helping to tend to her elderly grandmother. As we stepped through the door into the bedroom and started to grasp the situation, I was taken aback by the magnitude of medical and physical problems to deal with. The room itself was poorly ventilated, just the door and one window for air flow and light. Our patient, Lucinda M, was a 90 year-old female with a history of end-stage heart failure. She sat on a small cushion on the floor leaning against her bed for support. This was apparently her only comfortable position for breathing. She was markedly swollen, to the point of extreme swelling of all body tissues that is usually associated with poor protein nutrition and heart failure. She appeared moderately short of breath just sitting there and was quite weak. Her abdomen was extremely swollen from fluid as well. She sat there in nothing but a tank top shirt and underwear, with a urine catheter attached to a drainage bag.

She could barely talk for herself, so her son and granddaughter informed us of her needs. The catheter appeared to be blocked and should be replaced. As I looked through her chart, I also noted the question of a breast mass mentioned on her last doctor visit a couple months previous. Sure enough, Sister Emila had included supplies to replace the catheter, but I found myself feeling mildly annoyed at her for not informing me of this fact.

We had to shut the door to the room in order to better examine her, which made the temperature in the room even worse. Michelle had never seen anything like this and was not at all sure how to help me clinically to accomplish this task. The rest of the patient's examination revealed a considerable amount of fluid in her lungs, edema in her legs, and even some in her arms. Her muscle mass was markedly atrophic, and her right breast did in fact have a large firm mass, the size of a lemon. I feared this could in fact be cancer and even thought I felt some worrisome lymph nodes in her supraclavicular area as well. (Sorry for the clinical details).

She was already on a moderately high dose of furosemide to help get some of the fluid out of her body. She had numerous other medications, but it was very likely that she was not taking them properly. Her appetite was poor, and she looked tired. My assessment, as she sat there on the floor, was end-stage heart failure, with possible metastatic breast cancer, and swollen abdomen, possibly from liver metastasis or hepatic-renal failure.

The request to replace her catheter was not going to be easy to do, but I felt obliged to try. Her son and I had to first hoist her up onto the bed. I had to give Michelle step-by-step instructions on how to help me, handing me supplies for the process while trying to maintain some semblance of sterile technique. I had to fight my tendency to grumble under my breath throughout. We could barely get our gloves on due to the sweat already on our hands. Her son and granddaughter had to help hold her thighs apart, so I could deflate the catheter bulb and remove the old catheter. With some effort I was then able to re-insert a new catheter but was dismayed to see only about 40-50 ml. of dark urine drain out. Everything was pointing to a rather grim medical prognosis.

Michelle and I were, by this point, on the verge of tears and sweat soaked through our clothes. The next step was to get Lucinda dressed again and placed back on her little cushion. I tried as best I could, through my frazzled emotions and fatigue to explain to Lucinda and her family what I thought was facing them. Only a few adjustments would be made in her medications to try to make them a little more effective, and I promised to have Sister Emila get them a supply of pain medication should that become necessary. I tried to get across the facts of the case and help them appreciate that she had had a long 90 years here on earth, and they needed to focus on the inevitable soon transition to the next life. They seemed appreciative, but I felt inadequate and weak. I felt bad that that was all I could do.

As we walked out of the house and back down the path to the road, Michelle and I could not speak to each other. We got into the waiting car with Stanley and rode back to our clinic dorm in silence. Once there, Michelle finally broke down and cried for a good while. We both had to take cold showers to clean up and wash off the sweat and the tears to get ready for our celebratory dinner. Our emotions were completely frazzled, and I found it hard to be supportive and caring for Michelle, focusing instead on my own inner turmoil.

I spent the subsequent months pondering and praying about this event. Michelle and I had the chance to re-hash the whole situation and what was going on inside our heads and hearts. I struggled to discern what I should have done better. What I should learn from this experience?

I realized that first and foremost, I needed a strong lesson in humility. I was ripe for it. I went into the situation feeling just a little proud of all we had accomplished through the week. I was ready to sit back and bask and celebrate! I like being in control in general, and when things get chaotic and I sense a loss of control, I can get snappy and irritated and frustrated. I recognize, after the fact, how I tend to be self-reliant too often. I fall into the trap of thinking it is I who is accomplishing whatever it is I am involved with, and I can very easily fail to keep track of my simple calling to be His instrument, His vessel. God has such a greater vision of the true mission of the whole Church, and I only see a very dim glimpse of that. So, it would serve me well to constantly let Him be in charge. I could have and should have stopped at some point in Lucinda's house, and just acknowledged that.

For some time after this event I beat myself up for being less compassionate than I should have been. I knew I could not do much medically for this poor lady, and that left me with a feeling of failure. It almost seemed to negate whatever other good we might have accomplished earlier in the week. I know now that that is not really a fair assessment. Sometimes the task I am asked to do is not what it appears to be at first. I know I cannot cure a lot of diseases. Most of the time we doctors are just helping our patients try to manage or ameliorate the illnesses they face. Recognizing and accepting this simple truth helps me, and that's okay. Christ really just wants me to be His ambassador wherever He takes me. My physical and mental capacities are limited, and He knows that. That's okay too! But when I lose sight of that, and rely on my own talents to get me through a day, I tend to get irritated and grumpy. Just ask the folks who work with me on a daily basis.

I found out later from Dr. Jeff, that Lucinda had lived several more months before succumbing to her heart failure. He and others did what they could to ease my feelings of failure in her regard. Jesus has tried to reassure me multiple times with soothing consolations. He wants me to stop beating myself up. He has tried to let me know that it was still a very good thing to have gone to visit Lucinda and her family. We were obedient servants to the point of near emotional exhaustion. We did what we could. We visited the sick and comforted the poor, maybe not as well as we would have liked, but still, He has let me know that He appreciates our being there.

Remembering my encounter with Lucinda and pondering this in my heart over the years has helped me face subsequent challenges a little more willingly. Maybe still not as cheerfully as I should, but I am trying to work on that. She came to my mind a couple years after this when I first met Wilmer and Maria Luisa in Guatemala. That story comes later. But I think Lucinda was nudging me from heaven as I worked through that subsequent encounter.

St. Lucinda, pray for me!

When you judge that you have somehow fallen short, do you ever hear little voices in your head telling you that you're just not good enough?

Do you ever feel frustrated and inclined to quit?

Have you ever asked yourself why God presents us with such challenges and trials, and why He does so at certain times?

My advice is to take those feelings straight to Him in prayer and hash it out with Him. Trust His loving kindness. Ask for His wisdom and understanding. Let Him teach you.

1 SAM. 2:8, (PSALMS 113: 7-8) "He raises the poor from the dust, He lifts the needy from the dunghill to give them a place with princes, and to assign them a seat of honor."

PSALMS 51:17-18 "For you do not desire sacrifice or I would give it; a burnt offering you would not accept. My sacrifice, O God, is a contrite spirit; a contrite, humbled heart, O God, you will not scorn."

The Scales of Mercy

We would weigh the wrongs of life,
Those we suffer, those we do.
We would tally pain and strife,
All we witness, all we rue.
In carnal sense we cry for justice,
We feel a need for recompense.
But carnal vision sees not clearly…
We judge unwisely and unfairly.
The here and now is all we see,
And feel the scars of memory.
Our scales are selfish faulty things,
No healing comes from measuring.
Whether we ourselves or others pay,
Our weary anguish seems to stay.
But there is such a larger Truth.

It takes a miracle to find…
But miracles are just the thing
That He Who Is has in mind.
The Truth beyond our vision's sense
Our tactile, fragile narrowness-
He has a different set of scales,
We know so little of.
The weight of one small tear of sorrow…
The worth of one small act of love.
We do not fathom as He does,
Nor measure as He measures.
A simple humble contrite heart,
To Him is precious treasure.
Though we might judge, compare, condemn,
And hold ourselves in guilt and shame,
He takes our every seed of sorrow,
And weighs them on His scale of mercy
Against the balance of our duty,
He declares the tally clean.
But Justice now for Mercy's sake
Demands a different path we take…
To use His scales on one another,
In teaching Mercy to our brothers.

(September 2017)

Proverbs 21:2 "All your ways may be straight in your own eyes, but it is the Lord who weighs hearts."

Chapter 12

Everyone is Looking for You (Catacamas, Honduras, 2005)

After three years of trips to Nueva Palestina in the state of Olancho, Honduras, the local bishop decided we should move on to a different community. He selected Catacamas, which is also in Olancho, but a little further north. We still had to travel several hours east from Tegucigalpa, but the roads were in considerably better repair than the pot-holed trails they call roads we had traveled before into Nueva Palestina. The team once again came from the Austin Diocese.

The first day of our weeklong mission was to be held on the grounds of a small school in the town of St. Elizabeth. When our yellow school bus pulled up, the people were waiting. A lot of people were waiting. News travels by word of mouth in such towns, and our arrival had obviously been well announced. As the gospel of Mark 1: 33 says, "The whole town came crowding around the door." I now picture this particular crowd whenever I re-read this scripture passage. There were hundreds of people in a clump in front of the building where we were supposed to set up our clinic. So many, and so clumped that we could not easily walk through them to get inside ourselves to even begin getting organized.

These people were the typical poor people of third world countries. Some were legitimately ill and seeking much needed medical care, many were simply aching and tired from a very hard life, and just hoped for some pain relief or maybe some vitamins. Some were curious to see the show of the gringos who looked and acted so differently to them. Most had some material need and had heard that we brought medical and other supplies that might help meet some of those needs, but I know there is always more beneath the surface! Psychological and spiritual needs abound! If you read a few verses down from the one I mentioned before, in Mark 1:37, Peter looks at the crowd and says to Jesus, "They are all looking for you." How powerfully true this is in every situation! We often come to God in prayer because of some material or emotional need, when the truth is, we are all looking for Jesus, always, whether we know it or not.

Getting this crowd organized, lined up, and controllable was not going to be easy. They were all excited and eager to get inside. No one was willing to back up or let someone else go ahead. Looking around the schoolyard, we noted several other buildings that appeared unoccupied. A suggestion was made and quickly agreed upon to simply set up in the other buildings first, before announcing the change in plans. This was done in a matter of minutes and then the crowd was instructed to turn around and move single file to the registration desk across the schoolyard so we could begin our work. This made me think of the scripture from Matthew 20: 16, "Thus the last will be first, and the first will be last."

We had nurses to triage and decide who went where first, then doctors, dentists, and chiropractors each took their turn. Crowd control specialists escorted them from one station to the next for the visits. Finally, the patients would line up at the door of our pharmacy to receive whatever medications were needed. The facilities were much like those we had worked in before and soon the actual work was in full swing. Several hundred people gradually made their way through our makeshift clinic, and the final line at the pharmacy again became a clog by the end of the day. There was only one small door into the dimly lit room, so only a few people could be inside at any one point. The small concrete porch in front of the room did not leave much waiting room outside either. This did not make for the best patient flow scheme, but it was the best we could manage in that moment.

Our plan for the day had originally been to finish up and get back to our headquarters in Catacamas in time for a celebration of the Mass before we had dinner. But our plans were not looking too good in that regard. By the time we wrapped up the work in the pharmacy and packed our supplies back on the yellow school bus it was almost dark, and it was obvious we would be too short on time for the luxury of a Eucharistic celebration that evening.

As we stood there about to load ourselves onto the bus, I smiled a very tired smile at Father Pedro (Garcia), our spiritual director on this trip. I remarked to him that I was just a little disappointed that we would be missing out of experiencing the Eucharist that evening. He very wisely smiled back at me and replied, "I think we just lived the Eucharist right here today!" That statement has stuck with me for several years since.

What exactly did he mean by that? I have been reflecting on this for some years as well. Our Eucharistic celebration, the Holy Mass, is a sacred rite where in the sacrifice of Jesus on the cross is recreated on the altar for us to fully participate in the Paschal meal that He gave the Church at the time of the Last Supper. During this rite the priest sets bread and wine on the altar, holds his hands out over them and prays, "And so, Father, we bring you these gifts. We ask you to make them holy by the power of your Spirit, that they may become the body and blood of your Son, our Lord Jesus Christ, at whose command we celebrate this Eucharist."

As I watched closely one Sunday, I noticed that his hands were not only reaching out over the bread and wine, but they also stretched out in blessing over us in the congregation, kneeling in worship. We ourselves had all prayed only minutes before, in the "Holy, Holy, Holy", when the priest asks us to "Lift up your hearts." We respond, "We have lifted them up to the Lord."

Our hearts are joined to the elements of bread and wine on the altar. We offer Him our humble and contrite hearts. And thus, when we partake of the Eucharistic meal in communion, we too are to be transubstantiated into the mystical Body of Christ. And that does not stop as we exit the doors at the end of mass. He sends us all out on mission to be His hands, His eyes, and His ears. The Eucharist, that celebration of the presence of God in and among us, must continue into our daily lives.

So, when Father Pedro pointed out that we had just lived out the Eucharist that day in Honduras, this is what we were doing. We were bringing the true presence of Jesus to those people, and many of them were bringing Him to share communion with us as well. It was the Church celebrating the actual presence of Jesus. But of course, the challenge is to remain in His presence everywhere we go, no matter what we are doing. And in spite of all my failings, I still believe, "He will complete the good work He has started in us!" (Phil. 1:6)

Chapter 13

La Gloria
(A slum outside Saltillo, Mexico)

The aforementioned story brings to mind what I still recall as one of the most holy celebrations of the Eucharist I have ever experienced. I recognize that my measurement of holiness is really just a reflection of my own mindfulness of what God is doing in and around me at any one point in time.

Our Austin Diocese medical mission team returned in 2007 to Arteaga, Mexico, which is where my missionary experiences began in 1990. One of our ventures on this trip took us to a colonia or slum, on the outskirts of Saltillo. This humble community was named La Gloria, although at first glance one would wonder how it got its name.

We had very little to work with in terms of buildings for offices, the best available was more like a barn than anything else, but it provided some shade to block out the sun in this dry dusty location. The dentists took one side and set up their chairs, the chiropractors took one little room that had just enough space for a portable adjustment table and about three people at a time, and we M.D.s had spaces walled off by sheets hung on poles. It was sparse, but it was enough for our needs.

The crowd was not huge because this was a fairly small community. Thus, we were able to see the people and finish up by late afternoon. As we stood around and packed up our gear, someone mentioned that there was a small chapel we could visit if we wanted. This was a little surprising to us because we had not seen any chapel as we arrived earlier that morning. The local missionary priests (Fr. Von and Fr. Tiere, French missionaries who lived and worked with the people in these colonias) even offered to say Mass for us. Of course, everyone said that would be wonderful, so we asked them to show us the way to the chapel.

Just about one hundred yards down the dusty road, we came to a shack made of pallets that had been wired together to form a building. A tiny doorway led into the small room that had a partial roof at one end, and open air toward the rear. There were some chairs and a stack of broken school desks in the back area, and a small table covered with a simple tablecloth served as the altar.

We made our way inside and Michelle and I stood in the rear, actually standing on some of those old school desks in order to see over the people in front of us. I could only guess that our congregation that day amounted to about 30 or 40 people. The French priest, in front of our very mixed language group, said the Mass in Spanish, of course, but his reverence was so amazing as he led us in prayer and worship. At the moment of the Consecration, he elevated the host, and a very noticeable breeze blew through the building and over all of us. Looking back now I can still sense the Holy Spirit in that wind, "Behold the Lamb of God!" Receiving communion in this setting was indeed glorious.

I have been blessed to visit some amazing cathedrals around the world, including Notre Dame in Paris, St. Peter's in Rome, The Church of the Holy Sepulcher in Jerusalem, but the bare rawness of this tiny shack, this chapel of La Gloria laid out the essence of The Holy Eucharist in a way that powerfully impacted our little medical team of missionaries. The community was enthralled in His Presence and truly celebrating communion; a mysterious communion that did not end with the final blessing, but carried us forward in our mission, wherever that may be.

One member of our group, Dr. Nathalie F. was inspired by this experience to come home and begin raising money to help the community of La Gloria. She asked her architect father to design and build a steeple to be added to their little chapel. They also succeeded in building a small school on the site, which included a sewing class to help develop more marketable skills for the struggling young people. Her heart for the poor continues to impress me through the years.

John 17: 20-23""I pray not only for them, but also for those who will believe in me through their word, so that they may all be one, as you, Father, are in me and I in you, that they also may be in us, that the world may believe that you sent me. And I have given them the glory you gave me, so that they may be one, as we are one, I in them and you in me, that they may be brought to perfection as one, that the world may know that you sent me, and that you loved them even as you loved me."

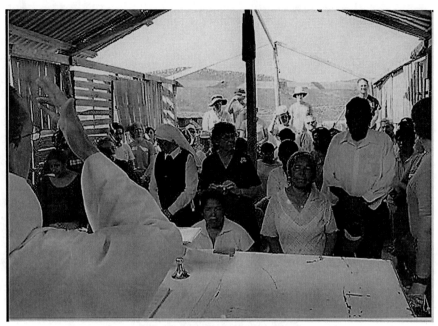

Mass in the chapel at La Gloria

An outside view of the chapel.

OH, GLORIOUS TASTE OF HEAVEN!

Down in adoration falling,
In thy Presence, rapt in awe,
For but a moment dimly sensing,
It is enough to heed thy call.

Bone of my bone, Flesh of my flesh,
Becoming one in holiness,
Knowing Love in sacred bliss.

Hallelujah to our King!
The Bride, enraptured,
Has to sing.
Love pours out, The Groom is Jesus!
Oh, precious One,
Consume and seize us!

Chapter 14

Oh Wow! Moments (Quetzaltenango, Guatemala)

The team of St. Francis Medical Mission of the Austin Diocese had finished another week of work. This time we had been to Quetzaltenango, known to most locals as Xela, a rather large city in the western part of Guatemala. Most of our days were spent in small outlying suburban towns working either in churches or schools. The team was quite large as we had six M.D.s, four P.A.s, a chiropractor, five dentists, several nurses, a group of well-trained oculists, three pharmacists, many translators, and a host of helpers. We spent our last night resting and being tourists in the beautiful city of Antigua.

As Michelle and I strolled around the plaza, bustling with locals hawking their wares, we found a bench and sat to take in the atmosphere. She posed a question to me as we sat there asking if I had had any great oh wow moments during the week. I had to reflect, as nothing had been all that obvious to me up to that point although there had certainly been some exciting cases in the group experience.

One of the doctors on the team was a young Mexican dermatologist who came with her husband, an emergency room doctor. This talented doctor not only treated innumerable rashes and warts, but also she had shown surprising surgical skill on at least two occasions. One involved a very large lipoma (a benign fatty tumor), which she removed from an elderly man's forehead. It was about the size of a baked potato and made it difficult for him to even wear a hat. The other case of note was a lady who had a nasty skin cancer on her cheek, near her nose. This had required a wide excision and then a skin flap to close the resulting defect. Both of these required considerable time (and bravery), and of course this caught the attention of almost everyone crowded into the little church where we had set up our clinic for the day. Cameras and recorders were going throughout her delicate procedures and everyone was amazed as they watched.

The people were truly blessed to have her there and willing to provide such expert medical attention.

At our nightly debriefing sharing session, Dr. Marta was coaxed into sharing her thoughts and feelings. I was even more impressed with her humility and compassion than I was with her surgical expertise. These specific cases would certainly qualify as what Michelle had termed, Oh wow moments. But they involved someone else and I was merely a spectator for these events. The question still stood if I, personally, had any oh wow moments.

The week had been very busy with hundreds of people lined up every day for their chance to see a doctor or dentist. Some were truly sick and suffering, but as usual, most simply wanted a check-up and to see what stuff we had brought that they might be able to use. We do try to bring as much as possible to give to them, and I don't want to minimize the value of some pain reliever or some vitamins to a poor person who can't afford to buy even such simple items. We were able to provide many diabetics and hypertensive patients with enough medication to hold them for up to a year. About 800 people left with a decent pair of glasses, and all the children who came were able to at least have their vision screened.

What I struggled with, throughout the week, was to fight the temptation to tally our numbers, and treat the crowd, rather than focus on the one person sitting with me at any given moment. The exciting diagnoses and spectacular cases were for other providers this time, and that is really okay! My task was to overcome my selfish need for control and submit in the midst of chaos to just do the one thing I was asked to do: LISTEN, intently and compassionately to one person at a time.

So often the litany of complaints starts to sound tiresome. Everything hurts, everyone is tired, and on and on, but each person is unique and deserves my attention. That sounds simple, but it is not so easy six hours into the day. I want to quit and sometimes I want to scream. Several times I found myself in midafternoon standing with one or two other providers at the entrance, looking out to see how long the line still was. We had hit our wall and needed to take a deep breath. We recognized our own fatigue, our human limitations. We would briefly commiserate and seek help, strength, and encouragement from one another. Then we would go back to our stations and get back to work for a few more hours. I knew when I signed up for this trip that I would not be in control, and I know I am asked to trust our Lord and those He has placed in charge of the details. This can be a real challenge for me.

I have mentioned before that finding some way to touch-base in prayer throughout the day really helps me. I like to find some simple way to do that, and I have shared some of those already. On this particular trip I had decided on a unique little prayer trick.

For the week or two before we left home, I had noticed that my glasses were getting loose and needed to be tightened, but I had never gotten around to that chore. Now they would be slipping down my nose numerous times through the day, and rather than grumbling under my breath each time I had to push them back up my nose, I decided to take that as a reminder to say the simple prayer, "Jesus, I trust in You." Doing this dozens of times throughout the day, really served well to keep me more mindful and prayerful through the week. I still grumbled some, but it was certainly better.

So. "Oh, wow!" moments? I'll share just one.

At the end of day four, as things were visibly winding down, I spent several minutes with a wonderful young mother and her four beautiful children. The youngest of these was a set of twins about a year old, Angel and Angelica. One she carried on her back and the other on her front, wrapped up in her colorful shawl. I delighted in her motherly stamina and the helpfulness of the older siblings. As I finished, I even took the time to get a group photo, thinking these were my last clients for the day.

As they stood to leave, I noted a young couple standing at my door. I took a deep breath and as I ushered the little family out, I invited this couple in. As I did this, I touched my glasses up to my nose one more time, said my little silent prayer, and asked what I could do for them. As is often the case, the last patient of my day seems to frequently present the most challenges. My translator, Henry, and I sat listening to her story, trying to grasp all the details.

She had severe headaches dating back over two years when she had suffered severe vaginal hemorrhaging which led to an emergency hysterectomy and then a month in the hospital in a coma. I surmised that she likely suffered a significant anoxic brain injury from that, but at this point her neurologic exam was remarkably normal. She seemed scared, depressed and in need of reassurance. I listened as intently as I could, and I asked Henry to probe even more for details I might be missing. On top of that I asked Sonia to come over from the pharmacy because her Spanish is so much better than mine and I hoped her feminine compassion would help Henry and I get across our concern for her overall physical, mental and spiritual wellbeing. Her calm demeanor and gentle touch seemed like a good addition to the equation, and I just wanted to be sure I had everything right and was determined not to be in a hurry.

This whole process took about fifteen minutes and ultimately, we wound up giving them some medications I thought might help her symptoms. But more importantly, we gave her and her husband as much education and clinical advice as we could. It was not something we were going to cure, more like something that just needed to be managed over time. We took our time, we let the conversation run its course, and we were careful and deliberate. In the end, I hope we helped this young couple feel reassured and confident as they faced their future together.

As usual, we were all paid in hugs as they took their leave. I felt like the simplicity of calmly taking time with them was my personal oh wow moment, as my normal nature I would have just handed them some pills and whisked them out the door. Something, (Someone) had made me relax and focus for those few minutes. No one took pictures. I doubt that anyone else even remembers that encounter, but as I write this, I recall my earlier encounter with Lucinda M. in Jamaica. A simple prayer that called me back to calm and compassion had made such a difference. Perhaps St. Lucinda was looking out for me! It was not anything worthy of a 'Facebook post', but that simple authentic moment of our connecting as a small church in that little room on the outskirts of Quetzaltenango was worthy of my personal "Oh, Wow!"

So, thank you, Michelle, for asking such a wonderful question. We could all do ourselves a favor by asking ourselves this question daily. In my ordinary day to day, do I notice the awesomeness of the encounters I experience? How has the Lord worked through me today? Did He? Was I listening to Him? Did I look for and respond to the "unmet need" in front of me? Did I miss the opportunity? Did I experience any "Oh, wow!" moments today?

Heavenly Haiku

Turn your face to Me,
My Presence is all you need.
Raise your eyes and see.

Chapter 15

Jesus, Tell Me a Joke
(Salem, Oregon and Phoenix, Arizona)

Not all of the messages I have heard from the Lord have been of the chiding nature, or even difficult to want to hear. Some have been light, happy and downright funny. Let me illustrate with one story from another part of my mission. As I have said before, going to foreign countries and volunteering for a medical mission is only one small aspect of the mission He has laid out for me. He has given me an even greater calling as a husband, father, and grandfather. On one post Christmas vacation we went first to Salem, Oregon to visit our son Michael and his delightful family, and after our time there we would proceed to Phoenix, Arizona to see our son Tim and his equally wonderful tribe. This trip provided a wonderful break from my work routine, a fresh new experience of the word holiday.

I am a man of routine and one of my routines that I found hard to break, was my tendency to awaken early, long before the rest of the family. So, in order to feel a little more productive, I decided one morning to take the dog, Annie, for a walk. She appreciated the attention, and I got some needed exercise as well.

The first morning was just a trial run, but I found it refreshing and invigorating. I noted a variety of birds that were quite different from our Texas birds. I even noted some wild geese honking their way across the sky above, and they reminded me of a video series that we had recently been introduced to called *The Wild Goose*. This series is about the Holy Spirit published by the Augustine Institute. *The Wild Goose* is an old Irish term that refers to the Holy Spirit. Seeing those geese simply served to remind me that His Holy Spirit is always present, accompanying us on our walk through life.

The second morning, as Annie and I walked down the same hill, I felt led to take a little more adventurous route and head up a different road that led to my granddaughter's elementary school. That would add another mile or so to the walk, but I went for it.

As we approached the school ground I felt impressed to pray for the children and teachers who would be returning to the campus in a few days. I had a sense of spiritual warfare and our need to pray for protection from attacks by the evil one. I wondered to myself if any other people were already praying for the safety of this campus. I decided to pray a rosary as I marched around the perimeter asking for guardian angels to be stationed there and for teachers and parents to heed their calls to fulfill their sacred duties for the sake of all those impressionable children, especially my own dear grandchildren.

I was not finished with the rosary as I completed my march around the elementary school, so I proceeded across the street and marched on to the high school campus, which was right there. I wondered, yet again, as I approached the high school, whether there were any spiritual warriors already praying for those students who were likely in even greater need. I again simply asked God to send His Spirit and to provide such necessary protection to this campus as well.

As I turned to walk toward the main buildings, there was a familiar honking sound. I looked around and was blessed to see a whole flock of those wonderful geese marching around the band's practice field, sounding like so many baritones in need of a few flutes. God's reassurance was palpable and audible. He had let me know that He was already there and that my prayer was heard!

My daughter-in-law, Sarah, later confirmed to me that there was in fact an active group of teachers and parents who made it a point to pray for those schools on a regular basis. But what a wonderful time I had being called to collaborate during the Christmas break.

The following day, Annie and I set out once more, with my intention to walk both campuses while joyfully lifting them up in prayer. The geese delighted me by yet again joining overhead with their unique honking hymn up in the heavens above me.

As I was about to finish my walk around the elementary campus and head back home, I noticed something stuck on top of the chain-link fence around the playground. My path was headed straight for this object and as I neared it, I wondered what it might be. That's when Jesus told me one of the best jokes I've ever heard.

I first thought it might be a shoe, then it looked more like a little doll, or a teddy bear, but finally as I got really close and could see it clearly, I recognized that it was a stuffed toy "Ewok" from the Star Wars movies. Just as I got up to it and recognized it, I heard Jesus sing an old familiar tune with a little twist, "and 'Ewoks' with me and He talks with me," wink-wink!

I laughed out loud. I could sense Him laughing along with me. I thought to myself, "Wow! You really get my sense of humor!" And He answered, "I know, I gave it to you!"

I just kept giggling to myself as Annie and I finished our walk home. Yet again, He had made His presence known to me in so many wonderful and surprising ways. It just seems to take a simple decision on our part to incline our eyes and ears toward Him. He is always there!

Matthew 28:20, "And behold, I am with you always, until the end of the age."

Moving on from Salem to Phoenix for a few more days gave me another opportunity, and yet another surprise. This one was the Blessed Mother. My early morning walks here took me up the hill to the elementary school, then on up to a pair of beautiful little lakes. I again decided to recite a rosary for my prayer. I randomly chose to use the Joyful mysteries. (The Annunciation, Luke 1: 26-38; The Visitation, Luke 1: 39-56; The Nativity, Luke 2: 1-20; The Presentation of Jesus, Luke 2: 21-40; and The Finding of Jesus in the Temple, Luke 2: 41-52.)

When praying, I do my best to focus on the Bible stories that are presented in each of these mysteries of the rosary. I try to watch the story unfold in my mind, listening for some new insight or meaning. I have to admit that I struggle to stay focused and often wander off into mental gymnastics and number crunching as I just try to keep track of where I am in the count rather than really meditating prayerfully. (Sorry, Mary!)

As I began the Fifth Mystery, I announced in my head, "The finding of the child Jesus in the Temple," (Luke 2: 41-52). I paused and wondered about the Biblical significance of this particular story. I mean it doesn't seem to quite jump out at me so much like the Annunciation or the Nativity. The question of why is this story so important to rank as a mystery of the rosary, hung in my mind for a moment. I envisioned myself posing this directly to Mary as I walked along. Then, ever so softly and sweetly she explained to me what this story had meant to her!

This was not really words, but more of an imparting of knowledge or a truth as she simply let me see the story from a new perspective. The fact that Jesus had been lost to her for three days, and then her rejoicing to find Him again in the Temple was a foreshadowing of the time that she would have to wait while He lie in the tomb for three days before His triumphant resurrection on Easter morning. This served to solidify all she had been told about Jesus by Gabriel, Elizabeth, Simeon, and Anna. As she searched for Him, she had to pray for guidance and strength. She had been told that

He was to be the Messiah, the Savior, yet at this time, all the outward appearances said He was gone, but on finding Him she was re-assured to hold on in faith even when we can't see just how things will end. As she went home and pondered all these things in her heart, the Holy Spirit consoled her and helped her know even more than ever that God's word is trustworthy. Even when all seems lost, He will fulfill His promise. Those three days would serve her well when she would have to wait faithfully from the horror of Good Friday until the ecstasy of Easter morning. Then it would be her time to reassure the disciples to trust in all Jesus had told them, even when they were frightened and full of doubt.

She let me see that the Holy Spirit is so often preparing us and teaching us, and we may not always understand until later when we are called upon to stand firm in faith to God's promises. I had the feeling of being a small child walking along the side of that lake with Mary, conversing casually, but sweetly, about deep personal matters. I was thankful that she had kept all these things in her heart and passed them on to the disciples of Jesus to help their own understanding, so that they could then pen them into the Holy Scriptures for our benefit. I was even more grateful for this special personal moment when I could sense her specific motherhood of me!

How have you experienced God's sense of humor?

Do you believe He has one?

When your mind wanders do you ever ask little questions and somehow hear Him respond?

How do you hear/experience that?

Chapter 16

Perseverance in the Day to Day
(The Mission back home)

In October 2015, the Austin Medical Mission group again went to Guatemala, but this was to Rio Dulce, in the northeastern part of Guatemala, and the logistical issues worried me. We had been through some rough travel experiences before, and honestly I was just not quite up for it again. Looking back, I'll just say that I am still at peace with that decision.

Perched high upon the mountain of my memory is the historic trip we had made to Bolivia in 2007. So many things went wrong on that trip that we jokingly compiled a list we called the "Stations of the Mission". On that trip, several of us commented about the poor planning, lack of safety, inhospitable conditions, and our disinclination to ever do such a thing again. And yet, most of us did in fact sign up for subsequent missions and have persevered either with this group or others. (There are more stories to come related to that Bolivia adventure!)

Nonetheless, I am amazed and inspired by my brothers and sisters who signed on to this particular mission to eastern Guatemala, as they did experience a good deal of hardship. One lady fell and broke her nose; another injured her ribs falling on a dock while trying to board a large boat that would carry them across a lake in the dark of night. Their accommodations were less than luxurious. The crowds were LARGE, and the return trip was delayed due to major weather issues, causing them to have to spend their last night sleeping on the floor of the airport in Guatemala City. But they did all make it back home, and the very fact of their perseverance lifts my heart and calls me to carry on wherever it is He leads me.

I have said before that such trips are working retreats rather than the be all and end all of our missionary calling. The true challenge is getting up every day and facing each day with its own set of stresses and demands. For me, personally, that means going to the office and seeing my patients, ministering to their real needs, and trying to navigate the ever-changing climate of healthcare in America.

But the more important mission I am called is to be that of being a loving husband, father, grandfather, church member, and responsible citizen. In every one of those aspects of my life I recognize how critical it is to stay anchored to Jesus and the guidance of the Holy Spirit. I realize that true communion with Him in everything I do makes all the difference between experiencing literal heaven on earth, or the hell of being alone, lost and hopeless. It is a daily, if not hourly, battle. I'm sure that's why scripture tells us to pray without ceasing. I felt His Spirit encourage and challenge me as I pondered all this.

The time we have between missions is often the larger part of our real mission! Be steadfast and aware of the spiritual battle we are engaged in, and never take this on alone. Take Jesus with you into every encounter. Be open to see and hear Him however He chooses to reveal Himself. Be ready and willing to be His hands, His voice, and His ears.

Matthew 6:10 says "Your kingdom come, Your will be done, On earth as in heaven."

Do you see your day-to-day life as a mission? A vocation?

So often we trudge through life, killing time, living for the next big event. A wonderful book by Fr. Albert Haase, *Becoming an Ordinary Mystic*, gives such delightfully simple advice on how to start living more in the present moment. Start by stopping and looking at the situation of your present moment, reflect (listen), and then let that lead you to a response. What is the unmet need of this moment, and how might you best meet it? He quotes Pope Francis (long before he became Pope) and a little bit of advice he offered his pupils, "Do what you are doing and do it well."

SECTION 3

Saints and Influencers

As I begin this section, let me just say that it is sometimes a bit of a struggle to start. My aim in writing is to simply help someone, somewhere, sometime, to open up his or her heart even if it's just a crack, and let the Holy Spirit in. That tiny inspiration is all He needs to do great work in us. He has reassured me that I do not need to worry about being eloquent or precise or persuasive, I just need to tell the story and trust Him to use it how and when He will. Your inner response to anything I write is unique to you and your situation. Even as I myself read back over some of these little stories, I am struck differently depending on my current mood or need.

The feeling that fills me as I start this section is one of utter amazement at the reality that is our Church. That is, the one Church, the Body of Christ, made up of all who know and love Jesus and are filled with His Holy Spirit. That is not a religious or denominational statement, but more a simple statement of spiritual reality.

As you read about the people in this section, I pray that you will let the Holy Spirit spark your own memories and bring to mind those saints you have known. So, here goes.

Stephen A Braden, M.D.

Chapter 17

Blanquita of Arteaga

My brother David and his family were blessed with seeing much of our amazing world during his over 30-year career in the US Air Force. One of the most interesting trips they took was a vacation to Calcutta, India. While there, they were fortunate to be able to visit one of Mother Teresa's hospitals. Not only did they receive a gracious welcome and tour of the facility, but also Mother Teresa herself happened to be there and granted them a short visit.

They even recalled later that my nephew, Paul, who was about 3 years old at the time, gave her his little toy dinosaur when she made a remark about it. What an honor it is to have spoken directly with someone who we now know as St. Teresa of Calcutta.

I say this as introduction to a story about another saint I had the blessing to know. Blanquita, who was born Blanca Estela Valdes Fuentes, lived in a small community called Bella Union, on the outskirts of Arteaga, Mexico. She was born on November 24, 1971. I first met her when I was asked to make a house call on our inaugural medical mission from Austin to Arteaga in 1994. I was not at all sure what we would find on this visit, but I went along with Fr. Tom Chamberlain and Dr. Anthony Manfre to see her.

Her home was a humble cinderblock and concrete structure on the side of a small hill up a rocky dusty road. We entered as welcome guests of her family who introduced us to the quiet but smiling young lady. Blanquita had severe rheumatoid arthritis and was so contracted and weakened by this disease that she was nearly completely bedridden. Thankfully, the family was able to lift her onto a chair to sit for some short periods of time. While there, we were able to examine her and then talk with her and her family about what might be done to help. Sadly, medication would only ease her pain somewhat. Most of her major joints (hips and knees) were so damaged that surgery would be needed if she were ever to get out of bed on her own again. Intense Physical and Occupational therapy would be helpful for regaining some use of her hands and upper body. These proposals seemed daunting to her family, but after careful consideration, Fr. Tom and Dr. Manfre suggested a a plan, and arrangements were made to begin the therapy at a local clinic with the necessary assistance of transportation and some funding.

When we returned to Texas, further arrangements were made with St. Joseph Hospital in Bryan where I worked. A generous orthopedist, Dr. Mark Riley, agreed to have her come for more assessment and subsequent surgeries. Once all this was arranged, Fr. Tom was able to bring her to Bryan himself and she was admitted for the first of several joint replacement procedures. Eventually she had both hips and both knees replaced. The PT/OT was indeed intense for her, but she was always smiling and appreciative of any help offered to her. I had the opportunity to visit her a few times during her stays in Bryan for those surgeries.

She returned to Arteaga and continued with her therapies and she made wonderful progress, such that in time she could get up and walk short distances with a walker. She also learned how to make rosaries and used this as additional therapy for her hands, but more importantly, this was a way for her to express her prayerful soul. She could not stay in the old house up on the hill where we had first met her, due to the inhospitable terrain, so she was given a small apartment at the church. Blanquita became a beacon of simple joy and humble service as she softly spoke the gospel to anyone who would sit and listen to her. Her gratitude was genuine and her message of prayerfully repaying everyone who had been kind to her was heartwarming and spiritually refreshing.

Over the next several years I was able to visit Blanquita a few times in Arteaga. Her disease, however, was progressive and as time went on the other joints, primarily her shoulders, fused into painful knots. She slowly lost ground overall and even with the best of attention and care she deteriorated physically. Her spirit though, was undaunted. Even as she returned to a bedridden state for the last months of her life, Blanquita was a smiling temple of the Holy Spirit. I recall our last visit as she lay in bed, with her steroid rounded face still smiling and speaking gratitude and blessings on us. She spoke of the graces and miracles she had experienced. She promised to keep praying for us, rather than asking for our prayers on her behalf. She faced death with resolution and joyful anticipation. I found it hard to speak much at all in her presence at that time and was more compelled to listen quietly to her profoundly wise, humble, peaceful, and joyful self.

Blanquita passed to her eternal reward on May 25, 2009. Our church recognizes saints through a rigorous process leading to beatification followed by canonization, but most saints never enter into such a formal process. We who have known such saints do not need this process to verify their authentic holiness. Some are called to worldwide acclaim and are well known for their works, like St. Teresa of Calcutta, but even she spoke eloquently when she said, "Not all of us can do great things, but we can do small things with great love."

This reminds me of my grandmother, Hattie Braden, who at 96 was also pretty much bed-ridden in her nursing home. She told me on one of my last visits that sometimes she felt a little sad that she was so dependent on others, and she regretted that she could do so little. But then she caught herself and said, "But I can pray! So, I just lie here in bed and pray for all of you. I guess that is something." Indeed, it IS something!

I am actively compiling my own personal litany of saints, and that list keeps growing. It now even includes my brother, David, who I mentioned previously. He whispered to his wife just before he took his last breath, that our blessed Mother had spoken to him and reassured him at that moment, "We're still making saints!" I encourage each of you to compose your own list of saints. I know that if you think about it, you will be able to recognize those with whom you have crossed paths, authentic apostles and messengers of Christ who have finished the race here on earth and reached the reward of paradise. They are part of the heavenly host that we can talk to and lean on for help and encouragement as we carry on ourselves. So, I am not jealous of my brother and his family for having the blessing of meeting Mother Teresa. Rather, I rejoice along with them and the whole church at the realization of how many saints are on our side, rooting for us from the choir loft of heaven. Let us carry on the work they have started, striving to reach that finish line with equal grace, humility and joy!

Santa Blanquita, ora pro nobis!

I challenge you to start your own personal list of saints. Who have you known who now basks in the glory of heaven? How do they inspire you now as you carry on in this world?

Stephen A Braden, M.D.

Chapter 18

Blind Faith
(Moncho Navaro)

Moncho. What shall I say about Moncho? His full name is Raymondo Navaro. He was legally blind, and had heart disease, and yet he felt a calling to come on several of our trips to Mexico, Honduras, Nicaragua, Guatemala, and Bolivia. Occasionally he even went ahead of the group to scope out the facilities in preparation of our arrival. He served mainly at the registration desk where his knowledge of Spanish was very much needed. But more important than just that role on our team, Moncho served us with his sense of humor and faith.

I recall one funny conversation we had as four of us sat in a small pick-up truck on a road heading to Valle Allegre, Honduras. Just to start a conversation, Moncho asked us each to tell our favorite word in Spanish.

My sister Celeste started by sharing her favorite word in Spanish, "Cacahuate", which means peanut. She just liked the funny sound of the word. We all snickered just a bit, but before the next one of us could come up with our answer, Moncho chimed in. He switched his own question around in mid-stream and stated, "My favorite food is 'salmon croquettes', but I'm not sure how you say that in Spanish!" Just the way he said it made the rest of us in the truck burst out in laughter. (Maybe you had to be there?)

I never saw him get upset, even though he was going through all the same hardships all the rest of us were experiencing. He just seemed to be blessed with calm and peace no matter what he was going through. When we went to Bolivia, I was concerned that an older man with heart disease might not be safe, considering the altitude and general rough unpredictable conditions. He did not exactly have the blessings of his cardiologist, but he insisted that he understood our concerns and felt called to go along one more time. It was another opportunity for me to practice my motto, "I am not in charge." Moncho loved to serve and the trips we shared gave him such a wonderful sense of being of service. He inspired the rest of us to be mindful of our attitudes and keep our own hearts focused on those we came to serve.

He loved bright colored clothes, ostensibly because he could see them better! So, when his heart finally did give out a few years later, we were all encouraged to wear bright colored outfits to his funeral. Another chance for us all to remember his joie de vivre as we celebrated his life well lived.

Moncho

On the road to Valle Allegre, the site of Moncho's "salmon croquettes" story.

Chapter 19

Candelaria
(San Cristobal, Guatemala)

Some saints have finished their work on earth but some of us are works in progress. One of such person I am sure is worth a mention here is Candelaria, of San Cristobal, Alta Vera Paz, Guatemala.

One of the fascinating aspects of going to small towns in Central America and spending a week serving our brothers and sisters with our medical missions is watching how the local people seem to catch on fire themselves and keep the spirit of the mission going long after we are gone. Primarily this is seen in the local church communities who jump in to help us from day one. They do all they can do to accommodate us and smooth the way for our work. Then they stay with us throughout our week, sharing meals, prayer time, and service projects and arranging for patient after care and follow up.

We noticed in Arteaga, Mexico, after several trips there, that the local people were really on the ball. Local service organizations like the Lion's Club and the Rotary Club pitched in to help the church and established some follow up clinics. When we were in Tamahu and Esquintla, Guatemala, for several years, similar things took place. Our feeling of being foreigners got less as we established personal ties with some of the locals. Their enthusiasm and generosity toward their poorer brethren and us was fantastic.

A wonderful example of this arises from San Cristobal. Not only did this community welcome us and work alongside of us all week, but also they eagerly sought ways to carry on after our departure. The local church body was full of life and ideas. Since we were blessed to have ample medical supplies to leave behind at the end of our visit, they wanted to find a way to use them to maximum benefit. We, on our part, had a few concerns because in times past at other locations, we had seen such supplies simply stored away in a warehouse where they frequently sat unused awaiting our return, often spoiling in the process, but San Cristobal was different.

One of the local doctors, Dr. Cortave, was willing to volunteer some of his time and expertise to see some of the poor people we had met during the week that would be needing follow up care. The church formed a committee of volunteers who would set up a room at the church compound to be used as a clinic and pharmacy. Other nurses would also be available to check patients who simply needed their blood pressure and diabetes checked in order to get refills on their meds. The local priests were enthusiastic in their support of these ideas. They recognized the need for a small amount of money to help fund this project on an ongoing basis and to supply some initial furniture and an exam table. Their solution to this small hurdle was simple yet awesome.

One of the areas we frequented during our visit was a small bathroom just behind the kitchen area of the church compound. It had one entrance in the courtyard, but another from the street side. This street is a crazy crowded madhouse on the market days with hundreds of people visiting town to sell and buy wares. These people have needs and the idea was to open the street door to these people and charge a tiny fee to use the facilities. All the proceeds from this simple project would cover the needs of funding the clinic project.

What really makes this special is the lady whose new job this would be. Her name is Candelaria, and she is such a wonderful gracious lady and she jumped into this new work with enthusiasm and joy. Not only did she find employment, she found her own personal mission. She now had a part to play in God's ongoing work in San Cristobal. She knew the profits were going to keep the little clinic running, she knew the people who came there would be treated with dignity and love. Her smiling face as the people come in to use the facility is in itself ministerial. Candelaria offered them a clean safe facility on those busy market days. She was always ready with valuable toilet paper, a splash of soap, and clean running water! These are not things to be taken for granted.

Even though we as guests had a few other options for bathroom use, I found it joyful to go visit Candelaria whenever I felt the need, if for no other reason than to see her smile and the sparkle in her eye again! No job is too small. She exemplifies the dignity of good work done for a good purpose. Like Mother Teresa said, "We are not called to do great things, but to do small things with great love!" Candelaria is also frequently taking care of her young granddaughter, who is no doubt learning a marvelous life lesson in human kindness as she too gets to help pass out soap and smiles.

In Mark's Gospel, Chapter 14, we hear of an unnamed woman who comes into the house where Jesus is at dinner. She anoints His feet with valuable ointment and causes something of a stir in those who held her in less than dignified status. Jesus rebuked them saying, "Let her alone. Why do you make trouble for her? She has done a good thing for me. The poor you will always have with you, and whenever you wish you can do well to them, but you will not always have me. She has done what she could. She has anticipated anointing my body for burial. Amen, I say to you, wherever the gospel is proclaimed to the whole world, what she has done will be told in memory of her." (Mark 14: 6-9)

This passage now also makes me remember Candelaria. She does what is in her power to do to further the Kingdom. She doles out soap and smiles to everyone as though she were doing so directly to Christ!

I heard years ago on a Cursillo retreat, as we went through one of the exercises, a simple phrase that is lived out in my knowledge of Candelaria. We each took turns, looking into the face of the other men on the retreat and saying, "The Christ in me sees and loves the Christ in you."

Amen! The Christ in me sees and loves the Christ in Candelaria!

Chapter 20

Sister Emila and The Three Teresas (Maggoty, Jamaica)

September 4, 2016, is the canonization date of Mother Teresa of Calcutta. She is one of the most well known saints of our day. She exemplified a life of humble service and dynamic spiritual vigor that belied her tiny frame. Her works and her words have inspired countless thousands to carry on and do likewise, seeking to serve Jesus in His "distressing disguises." My nephew, Paul, who I mentioned before, was in Rome to attend the great celebration there, while I spent the day in Maggoty, Jamaica once again.

Mother Teresa drew inspiration from her patron saint, St. Therese of Lisieux, known as The Little Flower. Her short life story was completely different from Mother Teresa's. She lived in France in the late 1800's, entering a Carmelite convent at a very early age and spending her entire ministry as a cloistered nun. However, she was gifted as a prayer warrior and an ardent supporter of missionary priests around the world. She had deep prayerful insight into the simplicity of just being who you are created to be and being luxuriantly content with that. Her authentic living out of that intention moved her Mother Superior to instruct her to write her personal story before her death at the age of 24. Her simple book, *The Story of a Soul,* is so inspired that a hundred years after her quiet life, she is now hailed as a Doctor of the Church. Indeed, her autobiography tells the story of her absolute love affair with Jesus. By not merely accepting, but rather embracing the simplicity of her calling, she has given us all hope of sainthood, in spite of our apparent faults and failings, or just plain smallness.

St. Therese of Lisieux was a Carmelite sister. She herself had as her patron saint, St. Teresa of Avila, the 'third Teresa'. She had founded, or at least majorly reformed, the Carmelite order several hundred years before. She too, was a Doctor of the Church. She, like the Little Flower, wrote her beautiful autobiography, in which she expresses in exquisite detail her journey into prayer. Her writings also inspire us to delve deeper into our own prayer life and give detailed direction on ways to do just that.

All three of these St. Teresa's call us to humility and service, and therein, eternal Joy. Although I have to admit the smallest twinge of jealousy toward my brother's family for the blessing of meeting Mother Teresa in person, I can quickly dispel that by reflecting again on how many saints I have been privileged to know personally myself.

Sitting here in Maggoty, on this day of worldwide celebration of Mother Teresa, I realized that we must first celebrate our own first-hand knowledge of yet another less well-known saint. She is still a work in progress, as I have alluded before, but I have no doubt that she too is a shoe-in for sainthood. One of the nuns living and working at the Holy Spirit Catholic Church and medical clinic is Sister Emila, a member of the Sisters of the Sacred Heart of Jesus. She had just returned from a summer visit to her native Poland, where she and her family celebrated her fiftieth jubilee as a nun.

After entering the order as a young lady, Sister Emila was first assigned to an outpost in Libya. After a few years there she was transferred to Bolivia, where she spent the next twenty years. While there she established an orphanage, scraping and scrapping with next to nothing other than her faith and tenacity. Finally, she was transferred to this little outpost here in Jamaica, where she carried on running this wonderful little clinic. She has had to learn several languages along the way, which makes for some interesting conversations. Every sentence has the chance of jumping from English to Spanish to Polish and back again. Luckily, she leaves out the Arabic!

The morning of the canonization, Sister Emila entered the church for Sunday Mass, and was shocked to find the whole community gathered to surprise her with their own celebration of her jubilee. We were blessed to be there for this amazing and heartwarming outpouring of love for her from this community. In each place she has served, she brought her own dynamic delightful little self. Much like Mother Teresa, she is tiny in stature but huge in heart.

Later, in the afternoon we journeyed on to Balaclava to celebrate with the Missionaries of Charity nuns on this wonderful day of the canonization of Mother Teresa. The juxtaposition of these two events brings home to me that Sister Emila is just as much a saint as Mother Teresa, although she would never admit it. Several people remarked on what we see each as a humble hardworking dynamo, as human as any of the rest of us, is someone obediently following Jesus wherever He leads.

Sister Emila on her celebration day

As an aside, let me add some comments about one more person. Father Vondrille of Saltillo, Mexico. This French priest was sent to Mexico as a missionary, and we first met him when we worked in the colonias (La Gloria) around Saltillo some years ago. His laughter and joy, as well as his respect for the dignity of the poor souls who lived in those colonias, was inspiring to me. Not only did he accompany us on that venture, but a couple years later when we traveled to Valle Allegre in Honduras, he made the extraordinary effort to join us there as well!

As a Frenchman ministering to Spanish speaking people alongside English speaking people, things sometimes got a little funny. He told us a delightful story of trying to learn English, and one particular lesson he had struggled with. His instructor had the class practice by saying the phrase "the three trees" in order to get the exact pronunciation down. That sounds simple to us but as he demonstrated his struggle, we all rolled in laughter, "dee thwee tweeze," is how I remember him pronouncing this phrase. Now, as I write about The Three Teresa's, I am reminded of his gently joyful spirit, and can just hear him struggling to pronounce this new phrase.

Sister Emila doing what she loves, cooking

So, as I come back to my original point, our Church is an amazing real and vibrant Being. We are not a group of individuals just clumped together at random. We are a single entity, a living Body. As St. Paul says, "so we, though many, are one body in Christ and individually parts of one another." (Romans 12:5)

Stretching beyond the borders of countries and the bounds of time, the Body of Christ is ONE. I only pray I will take my place and do my part and invite others to do likewise.

AMEN.

THOU, PRAYER

Thou, prayer on this beach tonight,
Gaze upon the gleaming waves
That drum with rhythm never bending,
Ever sending forth its roar
As though it were
The timepiece of the heavens
Counting off eternal seconds.

Know the sound of ocean singing.
Hear divine poetry of stars glittering,
Moon glowing, feathery clouds
Gently gliding through the peaceful sky.

Release all love within thy heart.
Feel! And fill thy humble part
Of God's exquisite work of art.

(1971- from a high school retreat at the beach.)

Chapter 21

Maria Luisa and Wilmer
(San Cristobal, Guatemala)

The St. Thomas Aquinas Medical Mission trip of March 2017 returned to San Cristobal for a fifth time. This one-week experience in the middle of Lent served as a powerful instrument of blessing. For us rich Americans, it served to bring us into closer communion with our poor brethren a thousand miles away. We are called to humbly put ourselves at Christ's disposal, to allow Him to use us to continue His healing ministry and the building of His kingdom. So many people have a hand in bringing this to fruition each year that it is hard to know where to start.

Those who work out the details of logistics, travel, supplies, housing, food, personnel, begin months before the trip ever has a chance to start. Those who support our efforts with financial donations and constant prayers are essential to any hope of success. The people who prayerfully answer Christ's call to join the team each brought their charisma and dedicated themselves to the task we were called to do, which included bringing our humble, contrite, broken hearts and offering them to our Lord to do with as He willed. He honored our prayers and blessed us in countless ways.

The travel issues went off without a hitch, well almost. Actually, Whitley did have to rush back home at 3 a.m. to get another vehicle and a hitch to tote our second trailer of supplies to the airport, but other than that, getting through customs at the Guatemala airport was absolutely amazingly easy! Someone, probably lots of some ones, must have offered up some serious prayers for that! From the time we landed until the time we pulled out of the airport on our way to San Cristobal was less than an hour! (Un)Believable!

Housing, food, and working conditions were all very tolerable. Weather was only a mild distraction with drizzly rain for the first few days. Our short hike to a local school at Niz-nic in this drizzly rain was supposedly only one kilometer, but some walking apps claimed it was more. That reminded me later of Matthew 5:41, "and if anyone orders you to go one mile, go two miles with him." At least we were being scriptural!

There are so many stories to share from any such experience, and I only know a few of them. The highlight of my week was once again related to the chaotic finish of the last clinic on the last day, but this story had its beginning two years previously when at the same facility, we were madly trying to wrap up the week's work and be on our way home.

That was when someone from our registration table came up to me and told me that there was another patient who needed to be seen. I was spent. Out of gas. But with some urging I reluctantly gave in and went over to them to see what I could do. There sat a lady holding a very small malnourished looking boy. They told me he was fifteen years old. I suspected the language barrier was playing a role here because he looked like he weighed less than twenty pounds, but he was in fact fifteen.

His name was Wilmer, and his mother was Maria Luisa. He suffered from some very rare genetic anomaly, which kept him from ever developing beyond the stage of a toddler. Although he had once been able to crawl, he could no longer do so. He could not talk, and he ate only spoon-fed baby foods. His eyes were matted and inflamed with infection. His muscles were wasted. Maria Luisa told me her story as she gently held him in her loving arms. She had no support, and she spent all her daily efforts to keep Wilmer clean and fed. Medical care was nearly non-existent for her, but I knew that even with all modern technology there was not much we could do to really fix or cure Wilmer.

So, I sat and listened. I held her hand and then I did my brief check-up and tearfully told my assistant to bring a few things to give them to at least try to alleviate his suffering. The love I witnessed as I sat there was palpable to my heart. I looked Maria Luisa in the eye and tried to express my deep admiration and understanding of all she was doing by just keeping her precious child alive for all these years. We cried together. I said a little prayer of blessing on them, and after explaining the few medications and supplies we had for her, we parted with a hug and I could not help but wonder how long he could possibly survive.

The following year, as we worked in a nearby facility in the same little town, I was busy attending a small family, when I overheard someone outside my make shift office pointing out to another of our team members an unusually tiny sixteen year-old boy. I immediately thought of Wilmer! I stuck my head out from my office to look, and sure enough, there he sat in Maria Luisa's lap. His demeanor was one of peace and contentment, and hers was one similar to the Blessed Mother holding the baby Jesus. Everyone who saw her sitting there had a similar impression. Some thought to take photographs and I was blessed to have my picture taken with them a few minutes later as we visited inside my little office space.

Again, I could only praise her for her very effective care of Wilmer. She told me he had survived pneumonia only a month previously and had been taken to a nearby hospital. But now he looked clean and a little more alert than I had seen the previous year. As I listened to his chest his little hand felt my fingers, giving me his blessing. A picture of that moment now hangs in my office back in Texas, as a testament of God's love at work. And oh, so many people have seen that picture and asked to hear the story behind it.

Another picture taken of them so reminded me of the classic "Madonna and Child" painting, that I asked my wife to frame one such drawing side by side with this real life saintly pair. As we were preparing for the following year's trip back to San Cristobal, I felt moved to have copies made of these pictures in hopes of being able to share them with Maria Luisa. I wanted to place the two pictures inside a greeting card of Our Lady of Guadalupe. I had no idea if Wilmer would still be alive or if there would be any way of locating them, but I followed the urging of the Holy Spirit and had the copies made and packed the greeting card in my luggage to give her as a small gift.

On our first day back in San Cristobal we spent several hours organizing our supplies, but then I thought to ask around to see if anyone recognized the people in the pictures to help me locate her. My efforts met with several negative responses, but on the fourth or fifth attempt, as I was about to give up, a lady stepped up to look at the pictures and immediately recognized them. She was a neighbor who knew Maria Luisa well. Unfortunately, she informed me that Wilmer had passed away a few months prior. She knew exactly where he was buried because it was right beside the burial site of her own son. She promised to deliver the pictures on my behalf and relay my condolences to Maria Luisa. My heart sank just a little, but at least I knew she would receive the pictures, and I prayed that they would be a blessing to her in her time of sorrow.

Later that night I shared my experience with the others on the team during our evening chapel time. I tearfully told everyone there of my discovery of Wilmer's passing, as many of them had seen him on the previous trips.

We went through our week busily working in more remote tiny villages. On the last day however, we were working back in the church compound itself before we would have to shut it down and load up for our trip home.

As I personally felt myself running out of gas and looking for a clock to tell me it was almost quitting time, I heard someone at my door state that there was just one more patient waiting for me. I continued with the issues I had to deal with at the moment- a young boy who had been told he likely had a brain tumor and needed to have an MRI and whose mother simply begged for enough money to cover that expense at the hospital. I turned to my doorman, Deacon Bill, (whose wife had died recently from a brain tumor), and choked up a bit as I asked him to take charge of an on the spot collection to fund this project. He nodded to me and let me know he would get it done.

I took a little breath to collect myself then turned to the lady sitting on my waiting bench. As I reached down to take her intake form and see what problems she had, I instead saw her holding the greeting card with the pictures I had brought. Our eyes then met, and I cried, "Maria Luisa?" She nodded, and we instantly embraced and burst into tears. That took a few minutes, but then we were able to sit and visit. She was deeply moved to receive the photographs. Her sorrow was still quite fresh, but as I tried to relate to her how powerfully her love for Wilmer and his simple sweet innocence had touched so many people in far away Texas, she seemed to understand and appreciate my efforts. That visit was a miraculous answer to my prayers. We both acknowledged that Wilmer now rests in Christ's ever loving arms, full of life and richly blessed.

I found out later that day that she had made an extraordinary effort to come to see me. The crowd outside our doors was too large to allow anyone else inside, and when the decision was made to shut down registration, one of our nurses, Chris, went out to at least distribute packets of vitamins to those who could not enter. She noticed this humble lady down on her knees praying and begging for attention. So, Chris was moved to kneel down beside her and ask what it was that she needed. Maria Luisa responded that she did not need anything, but just wanted to see me. As she said this, she held out the pictures in her hands to show Chris, who immediately recognized them and brought her inside to wait by my door. The Holy Spirit indeed works in wonderful and mysterious ways!

The theme for my week seemed to be tears, tears of wonderful joy, tears of cleansing, and tears of shared sorrow. Although I do believe that old adage that laughter is the best medicine, I also recognize that sometimes the medicine that is more specifically needed is to share our tears with one another.

Matthew 5:4 "Blessed are they who mourn, for they will be comforted."

Maria Luisa and little Wilmer

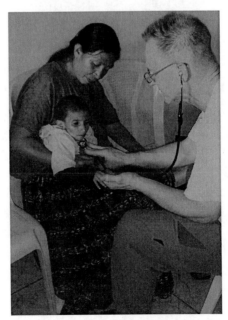

Maria Luisa and Wilmer

Stephen A Braden, M.D.

A blessing from little Wilmer.

In Mother Luisa's loving arms
The silent saint was held.
A tabernacle in the Temple
A dwelling place of love.
No word ever came forth
From Wilmer's tiny mouth-
Yet in his silence, In simple being,
Thus treasured and revered,
Without a word
The two sing out
God's song of love.
And in his sacred silence
Wilmer speaks to me,
At the very core
Of my own being-
"Lay aside complexity,
Worry, carnal limitations-
With Mother Luisa
Attend, with humble awe."

How glorious that
The sheer magnitude
Of his defects
Served to lay more bare
The simple sanctity
Of a being so well loved.

St. Wilmer, you have done
What was yours to do.
Even now pray for us,
That we may learn
To sing with you
God's song of love To one another.

Chapter 22

Influencers: Past, Present and Future

I recall my father-in-law giving a little reflection as he led us in grace before a family celebration some years ago. He referred to his family forerunners as a "great cloud of witnesses". (Hebrews 12:1). He pointed out, with heartfelt gratitude, that he owed them a tremendous debt for having brought him (and us) to this great day of celebration.

This idea came back to me as I thought back on the people who have influenced me and encouraged me along my own journey. Just the notion that I should see my whole life's journey as a mission has grown clearer to me over time. Some of my ancestors have articulated this quite well with their words of wisdom, while others have more quietly lived out their missionary call with such authentic enthusiasm and zeal that one cannot help but be attracted and invited to follow down that same pathway.

Certainly, my own list of the great cloud of witnesses begins with my family of origin. Parents, grandparents, uncles and aunts, so many it would be futile to try to name them all. Hard work, self-sacrifice, perseverance, humility, forgiveness, striving against the odds, falling down and getting back up time and again, all virtues modeled by so many who helped bring me through my childhood years into the more serious phase of the purpose seeking questions of teenage.

For a season, it was more often my peers who would influence my choices and behaviors, and I am, yet again, so thankful that most of those people were intent on making a positive difference in our world. Growing up in the 60's and 70's was certainly a chaotic and challenging time. Many of our generation fell prey to the luring lies of free love, do your own thing, and looking out for number one.

By far the most influential of all those peers from my high school and college days turned out to be my wife, Michelle. Our friendship and subsequent romance grew out from our involvement with an interdenominational Christian youth group. After a few years of friendship, when each of us felt confident with the authenticity of the other's desire to follow where Christ would lead, we began to prayerfully seek out answers to more specific questions.

Should we get married? I am Catholic and Michelle was Baptist. How would that work out? We were still finishing our college degrees and looking at grad-school. How could we afford medical school for me while she finished her medical technology degree? Hard questions. But each of us knew that our parents had survived very similar beginnings back in the early 50's. So, bolstered by their examples, we made the leap of faith and hitched our wagons to head on down life's happy trail together. That's just how it's done in Texas!

Talk of medical mission work occasionally entered the conversation during our early dreaming years, but as babies came along before I finished my training, such thoughts were placed on the shelf for a while.

Five years into our marriage God placed a different sort of mission before us. We were privileged attend a Marriage Encounter weekend retreat, and there our eyes were opened so much wider as to what this relationship of ours is truly designed to be. Living in a truly loving relationship, raising kids, being a part of a church community, and being open to sharing ourselves in that context became the heart of our missionary calling. It was during our time working with Marriage Encounter putting on future weekend retreats, that we were partnered with Father Tom Chamberlain to become a leadership team. Those few years did even more to solidify our vision of matrimony as an evangelical ministry. It also gave us a special insight into the personal down-to-earth side of the life of a priest. When Father Tom announced to us that he would be leaving to take on a missionary church in Northern Mexico, those seeds of our old dreams of missionary work were coaxed back into life. It took a few years for them to sprout, but it was Father Tom who urged me to consider coming down to Mexico to do a little medical work.

In April of 1990, my older brother Jim died suddenly at the age of 39. He was also a family physician, and it was he who had talked me past my self-doubts about becoming a doctor. Jim and Father Tom had also been friends, so Fr. Tom was very aware and sensitive to my pain at that time. Just a month after Jim died, I made a Cursillo retreat with the men of our parish, and the time to pray and reflect on the meaning of life was just what I needed. I was ripe for the invitation when Father Tom asked me to accompany him to Arteaga, Mexico later that summer. I was open, and just as importantly, Michelle was gracious enough to hold down the fort with our four kids to allow me to go! (She gets major kudos for that!)

Wow! What an eye-opening experience! I was just going to see where he lived and how he worked. I took very little medical equipment, just a box of simple medications and my little black bag. I planned to just get my feet wet, or so I thought.

Crossing the border at Laredo for the first time was interesting. I was not sure of the procedures or how strict the border guards would be. Was it even legal to bring my box full of emergency medications across? Would they confiscate them or arrest me? Father Tom's cool manner spoke of confidence and faith. Before we arrived at the border, he led us in praying a rosary asking for a safe and uneventful border crossing, and that is just what happened. At the final checkpoint, ten kilometers inside the border, we pulled up to an armed guard and smiled. He leaned in and simply asked whether we were transporting any firearms. When Father Tom answered "No." he simply waved us on our way.

I would learn later over the years not to take such miracles for granted. Border crossings can be a very trying ordeal. Sometimes it has appeared that our prayers were being ignored, but one way or another we always got through. We did the best we could with the supplies we had and tried over and over to learn the lesson of trusting in God's divine providence. This is such a hard lesson to learn and hold onto. Wherever you are, and whatever your current situation, trusting in God's power and care for us is the essence of our call to discipleship.

That first week in Arteaga with Father Tom was like taking an extended tour of a prospective college campus. He took me with him on his scheduled visits to the outlying villages, called ranchitos. The parish of Arteaga actually incorporates fifty or so such villages scattered over the beautiful countryside between Saltillo and Monterey. Many of the ranchitos only got one visit per month, with the larger communities were blessed to have Mass on a weekly basis.

On those first few days, Father Tom and I would arrive at a tiny chapel and mingle with the small group of parishioners before Mass. At the end of Mass, he would introduce me and ask if anyone wanted to consult with me for a few minutes. So, either at the back of the chapel or the back of his pick-up I would visit with a few people, check their blood pressure, ask a few questions and offer a few pills if I had something that might help. Great practice for my Spanish skills! I felt nervous, but I found their warm appreciative smiles and hugs very reassuring. Those few minutes of my attention were precious and valued by these simple hard working folk. I was getting my first taste of being paid in smiles and hugs, although frequently someone would invite us in for coffee before we had to be on our way to the next ranchito. They were fueling a fire deep in my soul, and I felt a desire building to keep that fire burning.

A little more stressful adventure came a few days in, when Father Tom suggested that I take the truck, accompanied by his handyman, Juan, and a local nurse, Micaela, for a day of making house-calls. He knew of several very poor sick people scattered in various ranchitos who might benefit by my visit. Okay, it felt like going from putting my toes in the shallow end to plunging headfirst into the deep end! I can still recall a couple of those patients in very humble homes in Huachichil and Los Llanos. They were so desperate for some medical attention that even though I felt woefully inadequate, they saw my visit as an answer to their prayers! When you can't afford to even drive the ten miles to town, much less pay for a doctor's consultation or buy medicine at the pharmacy, it must have seemed like a minor miracle to have this gringo doctor show up at their house and offer those simple pills for free. Father Tom knew his people and just where I was needed.

At the end of that wonderful week, I returned to Texas with the renewed vision of my calling to discipleship in general and my medical mission in particular. That vision keeps expanding over the years and coming into better focus. There have been triumphs and failures along the way, but I'm ever so grateful for Father Tom and the role he played in coaching me, and coaxing me, during that phase of my mission journey. We all have such people in our lives. Take a minute and think back on your own path.

How many of those "Father Toms"can you remember?

How have those folks helped you write your own story up to this point?

Let us appreciate and celebrate them.

MORE ON INFLUENCERS

This term has taken on a new meaning in modern culture, but it is not a completely new idea. We have all been influenced by the generations who preceded us. We are still being influenced day to day by those we look to for guidance. And whether you want to admit it or not, you are right now influencing someone who is watching you! (For better or worse!)

This whole concept seems to me to well illustrated by one of our mission ventures to Ahuacatlan, in the state of San Luis Potosi, Mexico. From the start, the fact that this little town even came onto our radar was the result of a humble gentle soul named Father Fred Schmidt. When he retired at age 75 from active parish work in Texas, he moved to this remote village where he had previously visited. He lived in the convent building of the little compound, helping the local pastor from time to time. It was he who got word to our mission group through his old friend, Bishop John McCarthy. And so, we took a little detour from our work in Arteaga in 1996 and went to Ahuacatlan instead. Ahuacatlan is an indigenous word for "land of avocados."

The team on this specific mission was a mix of seasoned veterans and complete novices. Most special of the newbies was my 15-year-old son, Tim, and my niece, Katy, who was a pre-med student at Texas A&M. She is the daughter of my brother, Jim who I mentioned before passed away suddenly.

The opportunity to have these and other young people come along was life giving and encouraging to us older folk. Tim had previously complained about how strict Michelle and I were as parents. He felt poor because we would not promise to buy him a car the day he turned 16. But seeing a whole new culture in Mexico, sleeping on the floor of the priest's kitchen, eating very simple but adequate meals prepared by the nuns, helping out in the dental clinic cleaning bloody instruments, all served to give him a well needed new perspective.

Katy jumped right in to help in the pharmacy handing out medications with an amazing mastery of Spanish. I never heard her complain about the conditions, but I found out later that she had been horribly carsick on the bus ride down there. She did of course excel later in medical school! She has gotten married and is raising her own children now, and they, as a family, ventured further than I ever did, by moving to Nicaragua for two years to work with the bishop there in Granada! I know that my brother, Jim is beaming in heaven as he watches out for them.

Tim also had the experience of finding himself something of a teen-idol to a group of young girls who adored this tall freckle faced redhead from Texas. They followed him wherever he went, and although he got a little annoyed by them after a while, I could tell how much it meant to him to be so esteemed. When he did try to find a few moments of privacy, they would come to the rest of us asking, "where is Teem?" It was heart-warming to see the effect on him and this rather new and unexpected aspect of our ministry!

I personally felt the influence that these young members of the team were having on me, but it wasn't until sometime later that I contemplated the notion that I was having a profound influence on them. Tim would grow up, join the Air Force, get married, and raise his own children while constantly looking for new ways to serve in his church communities.

Watching Katy and Tim now, it is easy for me to recognize how they are tremendously influencing their own families. It gives me such hope for the future of the church.

Earlier, I mentioned Bishop John McCarthy. He had been instrumental in our first efforts back in Arteaga and even joined us there on one occasion. What a joyful, down to earth man. When we were in Ahuacatlan, he stunned us all again by showing up to check on our work and the well-being of the elderly Father Fred. When he, Father Fred, the local pastor, and our own Deacon Jim Moat celebrated Mass in the local church, it was packed! The point was well made that our purpose for coming was not just to pass out some pills and pull some teeth, but we came to celebrate the family that is the Church!

We do not operate in disconnected silos. All we do or don't do has consequences. Someone is always watching. You are an influencer whether you have a million followers on social media, or just a handful of adoring little Mexican children!

Recognize and celebrate those who came before you. Acknowledge your current sphere of influence in whatever mission field that is. Understand that eyes that you may never even know about are observing you.

BECKY – AND OTHER PRE-SOMETHINGS

Tim and Katy were just the tip of the iceberg. So many other young people tagged along on other mission adventures over the years. In their experiences on these trips professional goals were formed or solidified. The deeper purpose of such professional choices became more real to them, as the concept of service took on a more concrete aspect. The opportunity to wash someone's feet, bandage wounds, assist with dental extractions, and otherwise touch the untouchables of the world has had profound influence on their careers as well as their hearts. So many of those young people are now doctors, nurses, P.A.s, dentists, deacons, priests, moms and dads! The ripples of influence just keep spreading.

In 2008 my daughter, Becky, came along with me to Dulce Nombre de Culmi, a town just down the road from Catacamas, in Honduras. She subsequently joined us on several trips to Guatemala as she worked out her own road of discernment. It was not always an easy road for her, but she persevered in her training and made it into and through the Physician Assistant program at the Southwestern Medical Center in Dallas. (My old alma mater!) Now she continues her mission work back home in Dallas, continuing her work as a P.A. while starting a family of her own.

Becky, Tim, Katy, Kelly, Lauren, Colleen, Jacob, Toby, Kim, Jessie, Haziel, Paul, Markie, Angela, Annalisse, Gianna, Celeste, Estefan, Ben, ... the list goes on and on.

Whatever tiny bit of influence I may have had on any of those young disciples, it makes me very happy and just a teeny bit proud to see them succeeding now. I marvel at the fulfillment of the promise to see a "harvest of fruit a hundred-fold!" Again, I challenge you to accept your important role as an influencer and do all you can to pass it on.

SECTION FOUR

Struggling to Hear Him in the Silence

Stephen A Braden, M.D.

Chapter 23

Bolivia, A Logistical Nightmare

In February 2007, the medical mission team from the Austin Diocese was on our way to a new destination. We had been invited by the leader of a small foundation called Angels of Hope to come to the small town of Villa Tunari, located in the Chipare rainforest region of Bolivia. This would be our first venture into South America. The logistics of travel were exponentially more complex than we had tackled before in Mexico and Central America. The flight plan started in Austin, flew to Dallas, then to Miami, and on to La Paz, where we would then hop another flight to Cochabamba, and then load onto a bus for a several hour ride down the east side of the Andes mountains and into the rainforest. Needless to say, the opportunity for hiccups was enormous.

Our team was made up of 30 diverse people. We had four medical doctors, five dentists, a few nurses, several college students, some translators, pharmacy experts as well as a 68 year- old nun and a 70 year old retired schoolteacher. Some were seasoned missionaries, and a few were newbies.

The facility we were headed for was a small school run by Angels of Hope. The founder had left Austin and lived at the site for about nine years, and they did all they could to provide food, medical care, and education to the young children of this impoverished area. This is about as much as any of us knew before the start of the trip. We would learn more and more each step of the way, some challenging, some outright disturbing. The lessons to be learned on any mission trip are numerous and specific to each individual's perspective and needs. And they just keep coming.

Even now, 13 years later, as I write this account, I am still processing and learning. I suppose I should/ could have learned many of these lessons years ago, but such is my tendency to be a slow learner. Or maybe, I'm just open to constant progression toward the perfection we are all called to! Yeah, that sounds better. I am aware that everyone on this team experienced the events a little differently than I did. So, as you read what I share here, please feel free to take it in from your own perspective. Maybe you have had similar experiences but found yourself responding in a very different manner than I. Maybe these stories will trigger a whole different insight for you. That's great. My own lessons and learning keep coming.

I digress, as we converged at the airport in Austin in the early afternoon hours of Friday, February 9, each person brought one carry-on bag and would check two large suitcases or trunks full of all our medical supplies as well as our personal items. The airport was crowded and having major computer issues, so just getting checked in was frustratingly long and already I could feel the seeds of worry starting to germinate in my mind. Would we even make it to the gate in time for the first and easiest leg of our trip? Luckily, we had arrived with just enough extra time and were able to get through security and to the gate in spite of the two-hour check-in procedure.

The flights to Dallas and then to Miami were relatively uneventful. We took off from Miami around midnight for the overnight trip to La Paz and arrived in Bolivia around 7 a.m. the following morning. The airport in La Paz is the highest international airport in the world with an elevation of 13,600 feet. The air is thin and there is NO time to acclimatize! Just walking out onto the jet-way to the terminal left us feeling shaky and out of breath. I was in relatively good health, but I worried about our older members, including Moncho, with his known heart condition. He had been warned about coming but chose to take the risk. But my worry seeds took another step toward sprouting.

The next surprise in store for us was going to the luggage area to find that a significant number of our suitcases had not arrived with us, twenty-two out of sixty checked bags. I started to pray, but the sense that I was not in control engulfed me not only emotionally, but physically as well. My pulse was mildly tachycardic from the lack of oxygen, my thoughts seemed a bit foggy, my mental prayers felt stumbled and like I just muttered, "God, please get our supplies here and don't let anybody have a heart attack!" The airport personnel tried to track down the missing luggage but could only promise us that surely, they would be on the next flight in from Miami. I was left to wonder if the issues back in Austin had caused the problem, or if there was just too much weight for one of the legs of our flight. Just not knowing left me uneasy.

Some in our group heard that the locals used an herbal remedy for the altitude symptoms, a tea made from coca leaves! Yes, that is the coca leaves from which cocaine is derived. This was for sale at small kiosks around the waiting area. Some people just chewed the leaves directly like a chaw of tobacco, but I could not go that far. We were at the airport for several hours waiting for the next plane to arrive, so we did consume a few cups of the tea. I can't say it really helped all that much. One could also buy some time on an oxygen mask at other kiosks, and I will say that that was more palpably effective for those who were more significantly out of breath and tachycardic. I was not too happy when one of the young, attractive college coeds in our group was whisked into First Aid by the airport paramedics to have her heart monitored, but not the elderly frail members of our group! I can still feel my jaw muscles start to clench just a bit.

Since we had a few hours to relax, some more adventurous in the group took a taxi down to the heart of La Paz to go sightseeing. I did not feel so inclined and just sat at the airport terminal. My wife Michelle went, and she took some beautiful pictures of the city and quaint looking Inca natives, most of whom expected to be paid for having their picture taken. That was a fairly nice outing for them except for one lady who had her digital camera snatched out of her purse.

We waited eagerly at the luggage carousel as the next flight arrived and the luggage started coming out, but we were disappointed to find our missing pieces were still not to be found. We were left with no choice but to proceed to Cochabamba on the next leg of our trip and keep hoping that the luggage would catch up later.

Arriving in Cochabamba, the decision was made to spend the night there in a modest little hostel and wait to see if the luggage would arrive by the next day. Those of our group who had packed their personal things in the missing suitcases were without toiletries or change of clothing. So, some of us spent our evening looking for clothing, including a pair of clean underwear for Marge, the 70 year-old retired school teacher! She acted appreciative but wasn't thrilled with the hip-hugger style we had selected! We were able to enjoy a nice meal at a quaint local restaurant, and even watch local bands practicing in the street outside for the upcoming Carnival (Mardi Gras) parades.

Back in the hostel, we had some adventures with the showerheads in the rooms. Some were equipped with a device at the showerhead to heat up the water as it sprayed out. Some worked ok, but some were tricky. Standing in the shower and hitting an electric switch to turn on the heating device proved moderately uncomfortable for Sister Lillian, but no real damage came of that, luckily. Michelle never could get the device in our room to work at all, so we just accepted the cold shower and tried to be grateful that we did not get shocked trying to make it work.

The following morning, we had a simple breakfast of coffee and rolls at the hostel before boarding our bus for the ride down the mountains. Word from the airlines was still indefinite as to where the lost luggage might be and when it might arrive, but we left instructions with someone to keep checking with the airport and get the supplies to us as soon as possible. Rumors also began to pop up from some in our group that even this bus ride was a bit iffy. Some people had heard reports of a landslide along our route that might cause some difficulty getting to our destination. But again, those were just rumors, and no one really knew how bad it was, so, we dutifully got on board with the luggage we had and started the trip.

I have to admit that the country of Bolivia is beautiful. Gorgeous mountains for the first couple hours, then lusher and lusher vegetation as we descended. A couple of hours into our drive we came to a military checkpoint, where soldiers opened the luggage bays on the underside of the bus and did their brief inspection. We were thankful that after a few slightly tense minutes, we were waved on. Shortly after this, however, we were startled to see some of our suitcases tumbling out along the roadside. Luckily, someone saw or heard this and got the bus driver to stop. Several of us had to trek back up the hill to retrieve the items, but thankfully, it was just a minor issue of not closing the doors to the luggage bays. No big deal.

Next came one of the most difficult roadblocks I have ever experienced. The narrow two-lane highway heading down the mountain had trucks parked along the side of the road. All of them were too large to do a U-turn and they appeared to have been sitting there for a while. We were able to get down the hill a bit further but eventually had to stop. There we saw the reason for all the traffic being stopped, a huge landslide had in fact occurred a few days before. I would estimate it to have been about a quarter of a mile across and it completely destroyed the road and even blocked the river below us. Bulldozers were at work trying to make a passable road for these trapped truckers, but progress was slow. The only way across was on foot through a trail of sorts above the landslide area. People were already trekking back and forth carrying what they could by hand.

Our host had come from the other side and told us he had another bus ready for us there, but we would have to tote our luggage across this muddy trail. We joked that at least this was one advantage of having 22 less trunks to carry over! Some of the locals who were literally camped out at the site with their produce-laden trucks were eager to have the offer of a few dollars to help in getting our things across. I began to notice a distinct uncomfortable awareness of something inside me during that experience. An us versus them feeling. We had money and connections and could just walk across (even though that was not necessarily easy) to another waiting bus and proceed on our way.

They were stuck for days hoping to get through with their trucks before all the goods they were taking to market would go to waste.

I also noted more uncomfortable feelings of resentment toward whoever was in charge. How could we have gotten into this predicament? Why didn't anybody know how bad this road situation was? Oh well, nothing to do now but trudge onward. The whispers of grumbling in my heart began to simmer.

Getting across the chasm of the landslide was challenging. As I mentioned before, some of our members were elderly and not in the best of health. Sister Lillian, in her habit, found the muddy path difficult but she kept smiling. Celeste in her comfortable flats found them less than adequate for hiking under these conditions. By the time she got across those shoes were pretty well shot! Jeff dealt with this by joking and smiling his silly grin all the while. That amazed me. I trudged along with my carry-on bag, grateful that I at least had my clothing and personal equipment. Trudging is a good word for this. The trail literally felt like a giant anthill, with people going both directions. The locals were carrying heavy packs and even children up and down from one side to the other. We slipped and fell as we wrestled our way through. Deacon Richard slipped once and grabbed a tree to brace his fall, unfortunately it was a thorn tree and he imbedded a rather large thorn into his palm. It broke off and we could not address it at the moment. It would just have to wait.

Eventually, we did make it across with our luggage still in our possession. What we had with us, that is. Loading onto the next bus, filthy from the muddy trail, we were at least on our way again. That's when our host, M.M., started to introduce himself and tell us more about his project. Something in his demeanor struck me as just a bit off. Medically speaking that is. He was somewhat grandiose and pompous, with a tendency to speak in constant superlatives. Maybe I was wrong, but I wondered if he was trustworthy from the get-go. I looked around at my M.D. colleagues and noticed similar concerns in their eyes as we made eye contact and wrinkled our eyebrows. I thought to myself, "This guy has not been taking his medications as prescribed!" Coming down the mountain had alleviated some of the altitude symptoms, but I didn't necessarily feel better. A haunting memory of the Jim Jones tragedy some year's prior floated through my mind. The flavoring of suspicion was now added to my simmering soup of worry, resentment and grumbling!

Chapter 24

Angels of Hope in Villa Tunari

We finally arrived at Villa Tunari a couple hours later. The bus drove through the typical small town of Latin America and about a mile further where we passed through yet another quiet little military check point and then into the compound of Angels of Hope. This was actually a rather nice little facility. The school focused on younger children, preschool and elementary, and there was a nice kitchen and dining room. There were rooms we could use for the pharmacy and medical and dental exams. The playground equipment was handmade and rather rustic but not the worst we had ever seen. An open courtyard in the center would be more than adequate for our purposes. The space seemed quite adequate and was clean.

Outside the buildings was an open area where they had constructed a little stage and folding chairs for us all to sit. First, we celebrated Mass, as it was now Sunday evening, and this would be our one and only opportunity to have mass together for the week. After the bilingual hour and a half service we got another treat. The children had prepared a welcoming production, so even though we were dirty, tired and hungry, we now were asked to sit and graciously enjoy the show. They were actually quite cute, and we were well entertained. At the end of the show we had refreshments of sweets and a warm drink made out of some sort of berry. When this was finished, we helped carry the chairs back into the classrooms, and finally, supper, which was a delicious bowl of soup, followed by some meat and rice.

As conversations ensued, we found out from some of the local workers that the last military check point we had come through marked the border of what they called the Red Zone. This was a highly patrolled area where the government was officially trying to stamp out coca plant farming. Only later did we discover what a politically volatile situation this produced. The USA wanted the cocaine industry stopped, but this was their biggest cash crop. It was difficult to tell sometimes just how welcome we were.

Our sleeping situation was another surprise. Two options were available. Just a couple hundred yards up the road was a nice little hostel (Castillo de Angeles) where most of the international volunteers stayed. Only about 4 rooms were available, so it was decided to have the doctors and dentists, along with my wife Michelle, stay there, within walking distance of our workplace. The others were bussed back into town where a not so nice hostel was waiting. The description we heard the next morning was simple cinder block rooms side by side with 2 cots in each room, a nightstand, and only a simple curtain for a door to each room. The shower and bathrooms were downstairs which they all had to share.

The international volunteers were from all over the world, and were mostly young adults who looked at this as an opportunity to serve, not unlike the Peace Corps. Some stayed a month, some up to 6 months. We met young folks from Ireland, England, Canada, Israel, and several other South American countries. They were sincere and dedicated in their work, not only at the little school, but also out in the community teaching basic hygiene and nutrition. They gave me hope for the future.

Our workdays over the following week all seem to meld together in my mind. The limited supplies in the pharmacy had to make do because we still had no definitive word as to when, or if, our other supplies might arrive. We did what we could to see those who came for consultations. Thankfully, the dentists did have enough instruments available to pull some bad teeth. We wound up writing old-fashioned prescriptions and leaving them on file in the office, so people could return later to have them filled when more medicines did finally get there. I kept praying that they would, but I just had this emotional quandary about where those prayers were going. It felt more like I was looking up to a sky full of questions, rather than being taken care of by God in the manner I wanted. I sometimes questioned, "Why is this happening," but struggled to grasp much insight. We had come all this way to provide medical care, and I had assumed God would take care of all these nasty little details.

On day one, the medical doctors set about trying to remove the thorn from Deacon Richard's palm. I watched several of the others give it their best effort, but to no avail. It's harder than one might think to find a small object buried deep in somebody's flesh. Ultimately, we gave up and accepted another defeat. We put him on antibiotics and gave him some pain medication but told him he might need a real operating room back home to take care of this adequately. Doctors don't like admitting defeat. As follow up, I did see Richard about a month after we got home, and he showed me the thorn. I could hardly believe how big it was! Where it was hiding and why we couldn't get it out is still a bit of a mystery to me. Certainly, another lesson in humility!

Dentist David R. had a small adventure one day in clinic. His Spanish is not too good, so he used a translator for help. As he was preparing to pull a bad tooth, he wanted to explain to the patient that he wanted her to bite down hard when he got the tooth out and he applied some blood absorbing gauze to the site. With his hand still in her mouth, he asked the translator how to say, "bite down hard", and when the translator spoke the words, the patient obeyed! OUCH! It took a few seconds to get her to relax and let go. So, I had another patient to take care of. His finger did not need stitches but still needed some attention.

Celeste did not get her suitcase, which held her clothes, so I wound up lending her an extra pair of my surgical scrubs, which worked out ok. Her shoes were another story. The simple flat clogs were falling apart after hiking over the landslide. Duct tape might have worked but we did not have any, so she got the idea to pull a pair of latex gloves over the forefoot to hold the sole on. This looked hilarious but did work ok; she even did a pedicure on the finger/toes for better visual effect. If you don't laugh, you'll cry!

Some folks went shopping in Villa Tunari for clothes with limited success. Tino found some military camouflage fatigues that did ok but reminded me a bit of Che Guevara. Some asked the ladies in the kitchen if there was any laundry available. Of course, they said they would be happy to wash some things for us. They took a load from those who requested it and brought them back the next day, but they were still wet. They explained that you just have to hang them out to dry. Unfortunately, we were in a rain forest and it did rain. Every day. So, in spite of our best efforts, the clothes never dried, and they wound up taking home wet laundry!

The rains also had some effect on our ability to see patients. We had set up benches and chairs for them in the open central courtyard, for the waiting room. But with each new downpour, everyone would crowd under the narrow eaves in an attempt to stay dry, a minor inconvenience. I had to remind myself that these people live with this everyday of their life. It is a rain forest after all. The pharmacy room was graced with a mascot, a rather large tortoise! He gently crawled about the room and offered us a reason to smile from time to time.

Finding reasons to smile was something of an effort for the group. I did marvel at Jeff's ability to get a small group of children together and teach them how to make balloon music. His laugh could be heard across the whole compound when they finally got the hang of it! I have witnessed this sight repeatedly over the years, in Mexico and Honduras, but for these particular children it was a delightful new experience.

Jeff did have his own thorn to deal with, however. On the 2nd or 3rd workday he received news from home, via a very limited telephone connection, that his stepfather had passed away. Although this was not completely unexpected, he and his daughter, Sarah, were left to deal with their grief two thousand miles away from the rest of the family. We could offer our condolences, but I again felt inadequate and frustrated for them. Wishing they could be with family was just that, 'wishing'. Sitting in silence together was about the best we could offer. My own prayers again felt heavy or somehow ineffective to me. I was impressed at Jeff's ability to accept God's providence in the midst of our situation. I am still working on learning to do just that myself even today.

Chapter 25

The Bolivian "Emergency Key"

The room Michelle and I shared at the hostel was nice enough. We had one key between us. The shower and bathroom were just down the hall, and everyone took turns with that. The first time I went to take a shower, I returned to our room to let Michelle know it was her turn, but I found her already out in the hallway, waiting. When I tried to open our door, I found it was locked, so I asked her for the key. She did not have it. She had not realized that the door would automatically lock when she came out, and the key was in the room. Okay, what to do? Across our hall was one of the Irish volunteers who served as sort of hotelkeeper for the building. Pudge was his name, and he was a typical jovial Irish guy. I knocked on his door hoping he might have a master key. Explaining our predicament, he smiled and said, "Let me show you the Bolivian emergency key."

Stepping across to our door, he raised his left foot and gave a very stiff kick to the door just beside the doorknob, and BOOM, the door flew open. "Not to worry. See how it works? Just don't leave anything valuable in your room when you're gone!" I was impressed, but still mildly annoyed at Michelle for causing this incident. Forgiveness? Hmm, maybe another lesson I need more work on.

So, next day, when the same thing happened again, I just glared at her for closing the door with the key inside. Not that it was intentional or anything, just a slip up, not paying attention. As the little vein on the side of my forehead started to swell and throb just a bit, I decided to try the emergency key for myself. BAM! So satisfying to see the door swing open and feel a little surge of power. Michelle was apologetic, but my graciousness was not equal to the task.

This happened a third time. Maybe it was just the wind, but somehow the door was closed again with the key still lying on the bed inside. She just looked at me. I don't remember saying anything, just BAM! Door opened and problem solved. Except my vein still puffed a bit bigger as I felt my jaws clench. I guess the lesson of understanding, forgiveness, and patience, still had more work to be done.

Every day the question would be asked. "Any news on the missing luggage and supplies?" Our pharmacy was running on fumes, and the stack of written prescriptions was growing with every patient we saw. We could do exams, offer counseling, pull a few teeth, and make a weak promise that medicines would be here eventually. But I missed handing my patients their medications and seeing those big appreciative smiles. Not that they were not grateful, they surely were, it was just an internal feeling I had to deal with; just another matter for me to wrestle with. I should have let myself be more inspired by the amazing Dr. Nellie. She was a dentist we had met back in Arteaga, Mexico. She had joined our missions and worked alongside us several times in Mexico, even bringing some of her dental students along to use the opportunity to teach. On this trip, she had traveled on her own to meet up with us in Villa Tunari. She did not have to do that; she just loved the adventure and finding another spot to offer her help. She had crossed the landslide unassisted then hired a local to bring her on the back of his motorcycle the final leg of the journey. Listening to her tell that story with a wonderful smile on her face, left me feeling a bit sheepish (or should I say 'goatish'?) for not finding such joy in the adventure myself.

Chapter 26

The Cubans

I mentioned previously that the political situation in Bolivia was unfamiliar to most of us on the mission team. We learned as we went. Shortly after our arrival we were visited by a small group of Cuban doctors who worked in a small hospital in Villa Tunari. They stopped by to introduce themselves and give us an invitation to visit their facility. It felt a bit strange to be asked to drop what we were doing and be diplomatic. Especially not knowing any more about the politics than we did at the time. Apparently, they were doing the required two-year government service payback for free medical education in Cuba. Bolivia was just one of the options they had. Our host, M.M., was eager to have the opportunity to get his toe in the door of the local hospital for the sake of improved access for his people who may need medical care in the future. He was hopeful that by us being graciously diplomatic toward these young Cuban doctors, it would improve his own standing with them. So, it was decided that we would take a tour later in the week to see all they had available at the hospital. I was less than enthusiastic, but dutifully boarded the bus with the rest of the team the following evening after we had finished our work for the day. The hospital was nice enough, completely donated, furnished and staffed by the magnificently generous Cuban government. We smiled and acknowledged their humanitarian efforts; our own meager efforts by contrast seemed small and even laughable, a dose of humility 101. We did our best to discuss options for referring sick people from the Angels of Hope school should the need arise in the future. They of course, were gracious to say, "Sure, send them any time". Our host was happy to get this done. I felt my forced smile to be yet another strain to endure. But I did become a little more educated in the process. Cuba is seen as the good guys in this country, whereas America is seen as nosey interfering gringos which was interesting and unnerving. After the tour, the Cubans invited our group to a party at a local hotel. Most of our team went along, but several of us returned to our compound to relax on our own. Five of us decided to walk down the road past the military check point to a small bar we had noted on our way in. We wanted a beer and needed to vent.

Thinking back on that discussion, I recall a lot of frustration on the part of all of us. Logistic snafus had abounded. We were feeling less than successful, and we were in what felt like a semi-hostile environment. The beer was wonderful. Our confidence in our leaders and our host was low to say the least. Information was minimal from day to day, and our plans for getting home even loomed as a foggy uncertainty. Some voiced the personal inclination to never come on such a venture again. I should add that in fact every one of us sitting there did indeed make more mission trips in the coming years. We discussed how things might have been done better, and how we would do things ourselves if given the opportunity. On and on until we felt a little less tense. The beer was good for that too. Then we went back to our compound, and got into bed, ready to face the next day.

Positive memories do warrant mentioning. Looking out to see one of our young college coeds, Jen, passing out drinks to those waiting to be seen. She was doing what was hers to do and doing it with a warm and gentle smile. Listening to Marge, the older retired teacher, sitting on a bench with some children trying to communicate with them. She knew little or no Spanish, so she just talked very slowly and loudly (in English!) so they could understand. Made me laugh!

Watching the local ladies in the kitchen preparing our rather good meals, so happy and chatty in their daily work. We had time to visit with our patients, as there weren't enormous crowds waiting to be seen. This was a blessing I tried to appreciate. Getting to put stitches in a young boy who gashed himself on the playground equipment was one of the few times I felt like I had accomplished something medical. But I even felt a little guilty for enjoying that!

I only recall one evening where we all gathered after dinner to do a debriefing, as we usually make some effort to do that on a daily basis on most trips. Prayer time was left up to the individual, and some of us were better at that than others. I admire Celeste for her efforts to sit quietly with a prayer book at some point in the day throughout the week. My own prayers seemed stuck on asking for solutions to logistical issues. There was little gratitude or praise or humble surrender on my part when I did try to pray, but there was the subtle feeling deep inside me that I was supposed to be learning something. But even that questioning prayer was met with a palpable silence, which I struggled to understand.

Chapter 27

The Journey Home

Finally, the day came for us to begin our journey home, and uncertainty persisted as to how this would go. Everyone boarded the bus after our last breakfast and we sat waiting to leave as our leaders stood outside having some sort of conversation, still apparently making plans. We were told to just sit tight and wait, but no information was passed along as to why we just sat there. I felt an urgency to get going. We had a long drive back up the mountain, and we would have to cross the muddy trail of the landslide again. The only good thing I could see was that we now had even less stuff to have to carry across. We had our carry-on bags and just six remaining red trunks to tote along. There was a plane to catch in Cochabamba and I did not want to waste any more time. I was ready to leave. Our team had all been given souvenir T-shirts at the beginning of the trip. As we had left our hostel that morning, I decided to leave mine with Pudge, the Irish key-master. He seemed appreciative, but I just did not want to take the shirt home!

As we sat there, I could feel that nagging little vein on my forehead now bulging in full force, and the grumbling in my voice becoming more audible to those sitting around me. We were crowded and feeling restless. Our quest for information was met with a "just sit and relax, we're working on it." At one point, dear blessed Moncho turned to me and gently put his hand on my shoulder to calm me. He made some comment about not having a stroke or something, and I just wanted to bite his hand. At last, word came that we were leaving. It turned out they had sent a scout up the road earlier and the report was not great. The road would be even more crowded, but we could likely get across. So, on we went.

When we approached the area of the landslide, we discovered that indeed the congestion was worse than the previous week. We had to get off the bus and start trekking on past those who were still stuck waiting for a passable road. We managed to catch a small break by cramming into a couple of small vans and getting a lift to within a half-mile or so of the actual landslide. I recall hearing a few less than hospitable comments from those people watching us gringos march by. I kept admonishing our group to forge ahead and not stop to engage anyone. At the actual site of the landslide, we were able to cross on a relatively flat area where the bulldozers had been at work. They were taking a break for lunch, so people were allowed to walk there instead of having to climb the muddy ant-trail up and over the mountainside.

Once across, we expected to have a charter bus waiting, as we had been led to believe, but that was not so. Our host simply set about looking for one. There were some buses coming back and forth from Cochabamba, but there was also a crowd of people wanting to take them. Somehow, we were soon boarding a bus and ready to get going on up the mountain road. The crowd did not seem overly happy with us. I suspect it was a matter of money talks, although I don't really know that. The best I can say for us in that situation was that we allowed three poor ladies with small children to come along with us because we had a few empty seats.

On up the mountain we went. The only stops along the way that I recall was to let off the ladies with their crying babies at some point, and again for dear blessed Moncho to relieve himself. He was obviously in extreme pain from holding his bladder for such a long time. He begged the driver to just find him any spot so he could go, but there was no good spot, so he finally conceded and let Moncho just step off the bus on the side of the road for a minute to do his thing. We jokingly told the near blind Moncho that there were plenty of bushes and trees to hide the view, but in fact there was nothing of the sort. He was just happy to have some pain relief. Forgive us, St. Moncho!

On the way back up the mountain in the bus, we had joked about all the little and big miscues along the way. Someone even had the idea to write up "The Stations of the Mission." As we commiserated everyone chipped in a new story here and there, and the list of stations kept growing. Michelle dutifully wrote them all down and shared them with the whole group at our reunion gathering a few months later. By then, we were becoming more comfortable laughing at some of this and less inclined to scream out in frustration. I'll include a copy of that list at the end of this section.

We made it to the airport in Cochabamba around 6 pm, and our flight was scheduled for 7:30. Whew! But then it was delayed until 9 pm. Once we did take off, the flight from there to La Paz was only an hour so we got there around 10 pm.

Our plan had been to spend the night at the La Paz airport and catch our early flight out in the morning, but at the last minute a decision was made to check into a rather nice hotel and get a meal and a few hours of sleep instead. So, we headed down into town, but the altitude was still very high. The hotel was indeed very nice, and a luxurious shower preceded a wonderful dinner. All was well until an hour or so later when the altitude sickness hit me and I was nauseated with a throbbing headache. I had to crawl across the floor from the couch I was sleeping on, through Natalie's bedroom in order to reach the toilet to wretch up the remains of that wonderful dinner. She was understanding and compassionate, but there was little to be done but suffer through it. At least I was not having any respiratory trouble. We got up around 4:30 am and headed back to the airport for our 7 am flight. It was of course delayed several hours. So, we waited yet again.

We did finally get back to Miami, through customs and on to the next flight to Dallas, however our flight from Dallas back to Austin was also delayed. Surprise! While waiting there, Jen decided she needed a cigarette, so unbeknownst to us, she stepped out of the building to have a smoke! That was outside security, so when she tried to get back in, she was not allowed. All the security staff had gone home for the night. She was stuck. Her patient and compassionate father, Joe, made a very generous and loving gesture by going out to her, renting a car and driving the two of them back to Austin. My own last few threads of patience might not have allowed me to be so kind, so I'm glad it wasn't my call to make.

On arrival back in Austin, we had only 6 of the original 60 checked bags. The airline would keep looking, but even then, did not know just where everything else was. We found out much later that the plane coming into La Paz to bring us back to Miami, had in fact unloaded many of those suitcases at the airport and left them there at baggage claim. One of the local doctors in Villa Tunari was eventually notified and he was able to get the medications to the people with waiting prescriptions at the little clinic. Hopefully the right people got the right medications and they did get some benefit from them.

Stephen A Braden, M.D.

Chapter 28

Lessons Learned

I was glad to be home and began to try to make more sense out of the whole thing. Years of processing and re-processing have led me to some healing and understanding. I'm not sure I'd say wisdom just yet, but I hope to get there eventually.

So, what have I learned? First, I proposed that as a group we owed it to ourselves to do better pre-trip scouting. This has now become routine. We could also do a much better job communicating as a team. I see some progress there but always room for improvement. For me personally, I struggled with the fact that such missions are not about passing out pills and other gifts, even though those things are valued and important. Visiting our brothers and sisters in need, sharing pieces of ourselves and our stories with one another is so much more important. Taking time to listen and hold the hand of a person struggling with miserable living conditions takes an intentional effort. Bringing a smile and a ray of hope for some respite from their physical and emotional suffering is a bigger need. We do want to meet as many of those physical needs as we can and we want to share the wealth and the blessings that have been granted to us here in the USA. We owe such generosity to God, but the greater purpose of our efforts is to spread the Gospel and advance the Kingdom. If we fail in that, then a few vitamins and Tylenol are not going to make much real difference.

I have since been able to read of some saints who shed a good deal of light on my pondering. Father Walter Ciszek tells his story in *He Leadeth Me*. He was a Polish-American priest who went to do missionary work in Poland before the start of World War II. He was later captured by the Russians at the beginning of the war, and carted off to prison. His story of suffering at the hands of the Russian KGB and being kept in solitary confinement for years after being captured makes me blush in embarrassment to even think this trip to Bolivia was difficult. He persevered in his faithfulness as a priest, reciting daily prayers and even mass in his cell for years, knowing that God is faithful and had not abandoned him. He knew there was more to God's plan than he was allowed to see. He held on to his belief in the divine providence of our Father.

Wherever he found himself, and whoever crossed his path was the situation in which he was called to minister, even if that was just to the interrogating atheist KGB agent. He makes the point repeatedly that each of us is where God wants us to be ministering right now. Recognize the unmet need sitting right in front of you, in the present moment, and do what is needed for the Kingdom right then and there. No need to question His providence, just trust and do.

I am struck by how often Christ greeted His disciples after the resurrection with the phrase, "Peace be with you." I need to hold to that myself. Peace does not require that everything be perfect around me. It is not a matter of comfort and being in control. It is a matter of trusting Him and knowing His abiding presence even when I can't feel it. My prayers should not focus on the "give me" style of the grumbling Israelites in the desert, who tried His patience, and did not know His ways. They had seen His works. But they would not enter into His rest, Psalm 95. I have been blessed to hear Him speak to me at times, but when I sensed silence on His part when I was in Bolivia, the problem was in my hearing, not His lack of concern. I was relying on externals and stuck in wanting things to go my way. This concept of surrendering to His divine providence intrigues me but is still a matter of daily struggle for me.

Sister Mary Bernadette Muller tells her delightful life story in *Sister Bernadette, Cowboy Nun from Texas*. The one quote from her book that really rings true to me is the admonition to "Measure everything with the yardstick of eternity!" Another passage from her book, "The memory of these experiences of contemplation give me consolation when the 'well runs dry' and I must plug along in pure faith without being aware of God's Presence—which is most of the time. The periods of infused contemplation last a year or two, and then for ten to fifteen years He is silent within my soul. Actually, it is in the dry times that one has a chance to prove one's love for Him. When all is going well and God's gift of experiencing His Presence makes all things easy that is one thing. It is also by His grace that perseverance is possible while walking the arid desert in dryness."

As I read over the travelogue account Michelle wrote of this trip, I noticed one other fact. She mentioned the beauty of the countryside as we traveled up and down the mountains. Not only the fabulous mountains themselves with the lush foliage, but the numerous huge blue fluorescent butterflies! I realized as I read that statement that I had missed an opportunity to intentionally trust in His abiding presence. On subsequent trips when butterflies became for me a gentle reminder of the constant presence of the Holy Spirit, I could smile and take a breath, and just relax for a moment. But in retrospect, even when my senses were telling me that He was turning a deaf ear to my prayers, the truth was that He was trying to get through to me. I was just too focused on my worries to hear or see Him. I was never alone or abandoned. God does not have a deaf ear. He does not require of us a mountain of faith. He asks of us just a tiny seed of faith. He will do the rest. So, when I can't hear Him, I have learned that maybe it's just the noise in my own head that is drowning out His "still small voice," (1 Kings 19:12).

I am reminded also of the end of the Canticle of Zechariah, (Luke 1: 77-79), "to give His people knowledge of salvation through the forgiveness of their sins, because of the tender mercy of our God, by which the daybreak from on high will visit us, to shine on those who sit in darkness and death's shadow, and to guide our feet into the path of peace."

Lord, please continue to guide my feet into your way of peace. Amen.

"He took him off by himself away from the crowd. He put his finger into the man's ears and, spitting, touched his tongue; then he looked up to heaven and groaned, and said to him, "Ephphatha!' (that is, Be opened!") And immediately the man's ears were opened, his speech impediment was removed, and he spoke plainly." (Mark 7: 33-35)

"An inconvenience is only an adventure wrongly considered." G. K. Chesterton from *The Thing About Fathers*

Chapter 29

The Stations of the Mission to Bolivia

1. The Gathering at the Airport
2. The Luggage is Lost for the First Time
3. The First Hypoxia at La Paz
4. The Thieving of the Camera
5. The Chewing of the Coca Leaves
6. The Arrival at Cochabamba
7. The Itinerary Changes for the First Time
8. The Arrival at the Hostel
9. The Shocking of St. Lillian in the Shower
10. The Falling of the Drunken Man at the Restaurant
11. The Quest for Toilet Paper and "Undergarments"
12. The Search for the Luggage at the Airport
13. The Descent from Cochabamba
14. The Luggage Falls for the First Time
15. The First Crossing of the Mudslide
16. The Piercing of St. Richard
17. The Burial of the Thorn in St. Richard's Hand by the Five Doctors.
18. The Crying of the Children on the Stage
19. The Celebration of the Birth of Luis
20. The Kicking of Blessed Stephen's Door for the First Time
21. The Gloving of the Shoes
22. The Miracle of the Multiplication of the Meds
23. The Serenade of the Balloon Choir
24. The Stitching of the Screaming Child
25. The Visitation of the Turtle to the Pharmacy
26. The Patting of the Panties
27. The Holding of the Toot-Toot
28. The Journey Through the Cuban Hospital
29. The Blessing of the Fried Chicken

30. The Return of the Toot-Toot
31. The Kicking of Blessed Stephen's Door for the Second Time
32. The Kicking of Blessed Stephen's Door for the Third Time
33. The Cursing of Blessed Stephen's Wife for Locking the Door with the Key in the Room Three Times
34. The Boarding of the Bus and **Waiting** for the Umpteenth Time
35. The Rolling of the Suitcases Through the Lines of Trucks
36. The Falling of the Luggage Many Times
37. The Cramming of the Team into Minivans
38. The Second Crossing of the Mudslide
39. The Appearance of the Bus
40. The Ascent to Cochabamba
41. The Bypassing of the Tunnel
42. The Passing of Moncho's "Water"
43. The Prophecy of the Steak
44. The Expelling of the Vomiting Woman and Child
45. The Waiting at the Airport for the First Time
46. The Boarding of the Plane in the Rain
47. The Second Hypoxia at the Airport
48. The Itinerary Changes for the Second Time
49. The Descent on the Winding Road
50. The Miracle of the Hotel
51. The Prophecy of the Steak is Fulfilled
52. The Retching of Blessed Stephen
53. The Waiting at the Airport for the Second Time
54. The Passing of the Imodium
55. The Changing of the Carousel
56. The Mayhem in Miami
57. The Waiting at the Airport for the Third Time
58. The Barring of Jen from the Gate
59. The Losing of the Rest of the Luggage
60. The Thanking God to be back in the USA

SECTION 5

Hearing God Speak Through Scripture

Chapter 30

The Authentic Lord's Prayer, A Reflection on Holy Week

I do not hold myself to be a theologian; my professional training is in medicine. But as a committed member of the Body of Christ, I know that I have been gifted by the Holy Spirit to do certain things. One of those gifts is the ability to take some little insight He shows me and articulate what that means to me for the sake of further building up His body. We are called to encourage, teach, inspire and challenge one another with that ultimate purpose. This chapter is added for that sole reason. Hopefully someone will read this and be inspired to delve further into the prayerful study of God's precious word. No matter how many times we may have read any particular scripture, He amazingly brings us more insight and clarity with each new prayerful conversation. Please take this humble attempt and pray with it yourself and see where it takes you.

Matthew's gospel gives us the beautiful Sermon on the Mount, covering three full chapters of Christ's earliest teachings. His authentic, authoritative Divine wisdom is manifest in verse after verse throughout these chapters. He begins with the Beatitudes and proceeds to address the hypocrisy of self-righteousness vs. true discipleship.

In the middle of this discourse, in Chapter 6, verses 6-13, he instructs His listeners on prayer. He makes significant distinction between self-serving hypocritical prayer with its meaningless repetition and many words, versusLi humble, simple, authentic prayer. He then proceeds to demonstrate how to do this by giving what has since been called "The Lord's Prayer."

Picture Him sitting on a boulder on the side of the hill, a gentle breeze wafting over the attentive crowd. He takes a quick breath, looks up at the clouds for a second or two, then closes His eyes and speaks in a soft but conversational tone:

Our Father who art in heaven,
Hallowed be thy name.

Thy kingdom come.
Thy will be done,
On earth as it is in heaven.
Give us this day our daily bread,
Forgive us our trespasses,
As we forgive those who trespass against us.
And lead us not into temptation,
But deliver us from evil.
(For thine is the kingdom and the power and the glory, forever. Amen)

A few short lines, but beautifully incorporating and encapsulating all we need to say in prayer. These words are quoted by Christians across the globe every day, millions of times. Untold volumes of study have been devoted to these phrases and all they reveal to us. Most of us will experience from time to time how a particular word or phrase will touch us or speak to us in a new way. Jesus Himself promised that *"The Advocate, the Holy Spirit that the Father will send in my name--He will teach you everything, and remind you of all that I told you,"* John 14:26. I believe I experienced this yet again during Holy Week of 2018.

Early one morning in the middle of Holy Week, I sat at our dining room table and prayed the morning prayers from the Liturgy of the Hours. Just a few days before, on Palm Sunday, we had heard the Passion read as the Gospel, as well as reviewed the story of Palm Sunday. The Psalms and other readings of the morning prayers focused on all the events of Holy Week.

Then, as usual, every time one does the Liturgy of the Hours, I came to "The Lord's Prayer". As I proceeded to recite these oh, so familiar words, I felt, or somehow sensed, I'm sure now that it was the Holy Spirit, that this prayer can be seen as a synopsis of Holy Week. With each phrase some Biblical picture flashed through my head. I had certainly never realized this or heard this concept before.

I subsequently found myself taking phrase-by-phrase and prayerfully studying Scripture trying to flesh out this idea. Listening to the Holy Spirit patiently guide me through this process was an awesome experience. It took me a few months, and included a one week stay in the quiet guesthouse in Maggoty, Jamaica on another mission trip to that lovely community. I used the wonderful quiet of that time to let the Gospels open up to me in a new way. The overall picture kept developing before my eyes and still seems to keep getting richer and more colorful as time goes by.

One major point that keeps coming back to me is that I need to try to see prayer itself in a different light, almost a different dimension.

When Christ first spoke these words at the "Sermon On the Mount", He was doing more than just telling us what words to use when we pray. They are not in any sense a set of magic words we need to utter for good luck, while holding hands, standing, kneeling, or whatever. These words, in fact, depict an intimate relationship between the speaker and God Himself. There is an initial acknowledgement and giving of praise. There is a statement of submission and servitude. We ask for very few things, but, oh, how essential they are: our daily Bread, forgiveness, and deliverance!

The difference I felt most powerfully was the sense that Jesus did not simply utter these near poetic words. Rather, during Holy Week, these words would be lived out! They would be effective, often in less than pretty or peaceful ways. There was a deeper sense of prophecy that became clearer to me.

I hope that by the time we finish this reflection we will see how we too may need to make this prayer more authentic in our spiritual journey.

Chapter 31

Our Praise

Our Father Who art in heaven, hallowed be thy Name

One of the first hints that Christ's sense of authentic prayer is different from ours comes at the very beginning of Holy Week. On Palm Sunday Christ finally arrives at Jerusalem. His entry is marked by joyous celebration, reminiscent of Old Testament kings, like in Zachariah 9:9, 1 Kings 1:35, Judges 5:10, 10:4, 12:14, and 2 Sam. 16:2 John 12: 12-14, Luke 19: 28-38, Matthew 21:1-11, Mark 11: 1-11 all tell the story.

The people proclaim, "Blessed is he who comes in the name of the Lord!"

But Jesus does not simply give lip service to His prayer. His intimate relationship with the Father and His absolute devotion compel Him to dismount as He arrives at the Temple- the holy place where the name of His Father is to be held in utmost sanctity. He walks into the Temple and proceeds to cast out the merchants and moneychangers, overturning their tables and even whipping some in His truly righteous indignation.

He shouts at them, "It is written, 'My house shall be a house of prayer'; but you are making it a den of thieves." (Matthew 21:13)

He cannot settle for meekness or timidity here. He must <u>act</u> to restore the "hallowedness" and sanctity of God's name.

John's gospel adds another part of this story in Chapter 12: 27-28, just a few verses further down. Some Greeks have come to meet Jesus and He begins to further explain why He has come to Jerusalem at this particular time.

He says, "I am troubled now. Yet what should I say? 'Father, save me from this hour'? But it was for this purpose that I came to this hour. Father, glorify your name." Then a voice came from heaven, "I have glorified it and will glorify it again."

Jesus does not merely say the words; He shows us by His actions the true depth of their meaning. He shows us the true fulfillment of the second commandment, *"Thou shalt not take the name of the Lord, thy God, in vain."* It's not just avoiding cursing, but honoring and holding sacred that name.

Thy kingdom come

Let's stay at Palm Sunday for a moment. Christ's triumphant entry into Jerusalem recalls the entry of prior kings from the Old Testament and this story is told in several of the gospels. In Matthew's telling he begins in chapter 21. Most of the people, including His disciples, had expectations that the Messiah was coming to restore the kingdom of Israel, in a purely earthly sense. But the next several chapters recount His further teaching about the Kingdom of Heaven in which He stresses time and time again, is the true Kingdom He prays for. His teachings in the Temple between the Palm Sunday entrance and the final preparation for Passover over the next few days are of utmost importance.

Jesus makes the distinction, time and again, between earthly kingdoms and the kingdom of heaven. Included are several confrontations with the Pharisees. There's the parable of the wicked tenants of the vineyard found in Matthew 21:43, *"The kingdom of God will be taken away from you and be given to a people that will produce its fruit."* When He tells the parable of the king who gave a wedding feast where the people refused to come in Matthew 22:14, *"Many are invited but few are chosen."* Or when He rebuffs the question of paying taxes by again distinguishing between earthly and heavenly kingdoms. In Matthew 22:21, *"Repay to Caesar what belongs to Caesar and to God what belongs to God."* Christ also rebuffs the Sadducees and their question about the widow who had married seven brothers in succession. I can almost see Him rolling His eyes as He explains, *"At the resurrection they neither marry, nor are given in marriage, but are like the angels in heaven."* (Matt. 22:30)

In Matthew chapter 23 He decries the hypocrisy of the Pharisees and prophesies the destruction of the earthly Jerusalem. In chapter 24, He talks of the final days and the final coming of the Son of Man. (Matt. 24:29-31- *"But immediately after the tribulation of those days the sun will be darkened and the moon will not give its light, and the stars will fall from the sky, and the powers of the heavens will be shaken, and then the sign of the Son of Man will appear in heaven, and all the tribes of the earth will mourn, and they will see the Son of Man coming upon the clouds of heaven with power and great glory."*)

Matthew 25 tells the parable of the ten virgins awaiting the return of their Lord, the Bridegroom, followed by the parable of the ten talents, and followed finally by the description of the final judgment where He tells us, *"Amen, I say to you, whatever you did for one of these least brothers of mine, you did for me."* (Matt. 25:40)

In these chapters, Christ makes such an effort to teach His disciples (including us) what the kingdom of heaven truly is. He then proceeds to take this lesson from a classroom setting into real life; a very physical living out of what will be required of Him in order for The Kingdom to actually come.

Later, on the night of Holy Thursday, He is arrested and brought to trial before the Sanhedrin, then sent to Pilate. Here, one last time, He warns the Pharisees *"From now on you will see the Son of Man seated at the right hand of the Power, and coming on the clouds of Heaven,"* (Matthew 26:64). When He faces Pilate, He is asked, *"Are you the king of the Jews?"* He simply answers, *"You say so."* (Matt. 27:11)

In John's Gospel (18:36-37), we hear a little more of His response. "My kingdom does not belong to this world. If my kingdom did belong to this world my attendants would be fighting to keep me from being handed over to the Jews. But as it is, my kingdom is not here."

Shortly after this conversation, Pilate gives the order to have Jesus scourged, and subsequently crucified. The soldiers proceed to strip Him, place a scarlet robe on him, crown Him with a crown of thorns, and place a reed in His hand as a scepter. They mock and spit on Him and beat Him. This is anything but a 'pretty' coronation ceremony!

When Christ prays *"Thy kingdom come,"* He knows exactly what those words entail for Him personally, and yet He goes on…

Thy Will be done, on earth as it is in heaven

Let's focus now on the Garden of Gethsemane. As Christ enters into prayer here, He repeats a phrase that echoes one He had uttered in the Sermon on the Mount, in Matthew 26: 39. *"Father, if it is possible, let this cup pass from me, yet,* **not as I will, but as you will.***"* The imminent reality of what this means for Him brings Him to absolute agony.

The will of the Father is, and always has been, that "You will be my people, and I will be your God." This has been written repeatedly throughout the Old Testament. Yet the people had failed so pitifully that He had the choice to either abandon us to our forsaken condition, or, come to us in physical form and atone for us Himself out of pure love and mercy, to redeem us and bring us back unto Himself.

This was the will of the Father. That we should know the unfailing love He has for us; that we should be spared our deserved destruction. That this love would be expressed on earth as it is in heaven. This required of Jesus, the God-made-man that He offer Himself on the cross for our sake.

He repeats this same phrase, "Not My will, but yours be done," three times in Matthew 26: 39-44. The truth and awful reality of His prayer soon moved from the arena of words into the physical living it out in His Passion.

Chapter 32

Our Petitions

Give us this day our daily bread

Go back just a few hours, to the setting of the Last Supper. (Matt. 26:26) "While they were eating, Jesus took bread, said the blessing, broke it, and giving it to his disciples, said, 'Take and eat; this is my Body.'"

God has always been about the business of providing daily bread for His people. Throughout the Old Testament we hear such stories, most famously the provision of manna from heaven provided to the Israelites as they wandered through the desert.

Jesus Himself had seen the need of the crowd of people He was preaching to, and on two separate occasions provided miraculous bread for them to eat.

But here, at the Last Super, He again takes us from the simple meaning of "give us food for our bodies" to the much more profound spiritual reality of "give us the Bread of Life."

In John chapter 6, we hear first of one of those miraculous multiplication of the loaves to feed five thousand people, but soon after this, Jesus gives His discourse on "the Bread of Life". (John 6:48-51)

When Jesus institutes the sacrament of Holy Communion at the Last Supper, our minds will once again be boggled, but He does not mince His words. He is giving us Himself, in the physical form of bread, to take into ourselves, thereby incorporating His Spirit into our beings with the intent that we too shall be "transubstantiated" into the Body of Christ, and have eternal life being one with Him.

One more thing I noted, He also feeds us with His Word. At the beginning of His ministry Christ quoted from Deuteronomy as He was tempted by Satan, *"It is not by bread alone that people live, but by all that comes forth from the mouth of the Lord."*

In John's Gospel, right after the institution of the first Holy Communion, Judas leaves to "do what he has to do," and Jesus proceeds to give us His final discourse. There are four uninterrupted chapters of His instructions to the disciples and His prayer for us. Already having fed them with His Holy Body, He continues to lavish upon them a banquet of His words. Indeed, they are about to enter into a time of apparent devastation and will need every morsel of this Bread to sustain them.

Forgive us our trespasses as we forgive those who trespass against us

The ugly depth of our trespasses and the magnitude of God's mercy toward us are impossible for us to fathom.

When Jesus has already been brutally scourged, crowned with thorns, forced to drag His cross up Calvary's hill, He is nailed to the cross; and yet in Luke 23:34 He says, *"Father forgive them; they know not what they do."* He is hearing the people sneering and mocking Him, and He prays for those very people!

Here we now also see the conversation with the two criminals who are being crucified on either side of Jesus. "Now one of the criminals hanging there reviled Jesus, saying, "Are you not the Messiah? Save Yourself and us!" The other, however, rebuking him said in reply, "Have you no fear of God, for you are subject to the same condemnation? And indeed, we have been condemned justly, the sentence we received corresponds to our crimes, but this man has done nothing criminal. Then he said, "Jesus, remember me when You come into your kingdom" He replied to him, "Amen I say to you, today you will be with me in Paradise!"" (Luke 23:39-43) At the very moment of His absolute agony on the cross, Jesus extends mercy and grace to this repentant sinner.

So often, as we fly through the recitation of this prayer, we barely take it to heart enough to try and forgive even the little things that others do to upset our peaceful, comfortable days. Can I even forgive those who drive too slowly in front of me, or the newspaper delivery person who forgot us yet again? We struggle with such little petty trespasses, but if we want God's forgiveness, He demands that we likewise show mercy.

If Jesus on the cross can forgive those who have tortured His Body and forgave us whose sin has made this necessary, how much more should we be willing to forgive others ourselves? Pray these words carefully and be mindful the next time you find yourself being judgmental, critical, or condemning!

Lead us not into temptation

Let us return for a bit to the Garden of Gethsemane. Jesus has entered into His prayer in the Garden, and the first time He turned back to His disciples He finds them sleeping. He says, *"so you could not keep watch with me for one hour? Keep watching and praying, that you may not enter into temptation. The spirit is willing, but the flesh is weak."* (Matt. 26:40)

Jesus is praying, really praying, to the point of sweating blood; and the disciples sleep. His angels minister to Him, as He knows Satan is about to take his best shot. When temptation comes our way, how fervently do we pray? I know personally that the simplest of sincere prayer on my part when I ask for actual grace to withstand temptation is indeed effective. I have never sweated blood. I, in fact, find it hard to concentrate in prayer for an hour. I see the truth of my spirit being willing, but I am painfully aware of my weakness both physically and mentally. I need to pray much more fervently to withstand the subtle and not so subtle snares the devil lay out before me. Regular, disciplined, intentional prayer to be spared or saved from temptation would do us all good.

Deliver us from the evil one

From before the dawn of the human race, Satan has made his choice. He turned away from God and made it his sole purpose to destroy the intention of God to live in perfect loving unity with mankind. The evil one started with Adam and Eve, and even now continues to prowl about the world seeking the ruin of souls. Each of us has fallen into sin and thus deserves eternal damnation. But Jesus' sole purpose in coming to earth was to thwart the evil one and redeem the human race. His passion and death are the price He paid. Exactly what transpired in the spiritual realm as those historical facts were played out is awesome to even try to comprehend. It's even harder for me to understand what Jesus did in the spiritual realm between the time of His crucifixion and His resurrection. I do believe in some sense He marched into the gates of hell and made it clear to Satan that He had paid the price for us. We are ransomed, and now belong to Jesus. This gift has already been bought and paid for. But we still have to accept it. God, in His perfect love, will not force us to love Him. But I believe once we open our eyes to know Him, we will not be able to choose not to love Him.

For Thine is the kingdom, the power, and the glory, now and forever, Amen!

This phrase is parenthesized in my Bible because it was not included in some of the earliest manuscripts. But for the sake of completion let's look at it for a minute.

After Jesus' death and descent into hell, He turned around and marched out victorious on Easter morning. This triumphant return far out shadows the previous Sunday, when the people simply waved their palm branches as He rode His donkey into

Jerusalem. Now, the angels roll back the stone from the tomb and He walks out in glory. The soldiers standing guard are left shaking in fear of Him and become like dead men. The battle is won. The Kingdom is secured. Death is defeated.

Let us not take lightly the magnitude of being invited into this Kingdom, to witness His glory and power. This is why He made us. This is how much He loves us. This is Who He is!

As we contemplate the Lord's Prayer in this light may our own hearts be enlivened, encouraged, empowered, and renewed. May we too recognize how we are called to live and know that these words must compel us to action, to take up our own daily crosses and participate in God's work here and now. Let me also recommend to you one of those many treatises written on the Lord's Prayer. This one is written by Fr. Albert Haase, OFM, whom I have referred to earlier. His book, *Living the Lord's Prayer, The Way of the Disciple*, is a much more in-depth exploration of this topic.

But for now, this is my own humble offering. Just meditate a little more intently as you say these words, especially during Lent. Try if you will, to picture yourself reciting these words while holding Jesus' hand and knowing what the fulfillment of each phrase entails for Him. Grasp how authentically He speaks to Our Father. Try even further to say the words more authentically yourself.

Listening to God in Holy Scripture is one of the most obvious and powerful ways we can hear Him. The practice of "Lectio divina" is a marvelous habit we can all try. Reading, re-reading, praying and listening to the living Word is something I know I need even more now as I approach my elder years. New lessons apply now. A new mission awaits me as I enter the retirement phase of my life. The mission of my family and local community is paramount, even as I look for more trips back to Guatemala and Jamaica. Hearing and discerning is ever more crucial. Again, this particular reflection is yours to enjoy, but more important is the concept of taking Scripture as His living Word, and letting it speak to you in the nitty-gritty, day-to-day life you are experiencing right now.

Section 6

In Summary

Chapter 33

Final Thoughts

What are the "take home" messages from all these little reflections? The poem, "I AM", at the beginning of this book offers a decent summary. God is always trying to make himself known to us. He speaks in so many different ways. I can only write about a few of the ways He has actually gotten through to me. Scripture mentions so many more ways that to me still seem nearly incredible--like the burning bush, the pillar of fire, the booming voice out of a cloud, or even in the dreams of St. Joseph.

I have experienced a marvelous variety myself, and I continue to try to make myself more open to His loving voice.

In the sacred Noise of Nueva Palestina, Honduras, I heard the Holy Spirit audible within the cacophony of a community being what the Church is called to be. Hearts crying out their needs, others responding in compassion, and hands working to meet so many of those needs. I've heard this same sacred Noise even back home in Bryan, Texas, when our parish busily packs up Thanksgiving food for the poor neighbors of our community.

I've learned to recognize the sacred Noise of a baby crying in church. Rather than letting that be an irritating distraction to my personal prayer, I try now to hear the more "perfect praise" (Psalm 8:2) of that baby being wonderfully honest in expressing his total dependence on God's providence.

Surely not all noise is so sacred. This world has plenty of very distracting and irksome noise. It's so common that we let our phones, TV, radios blare away at us, drowning out that "still small voice" (1 Kings 19:13) of the Spirit.

The noise of my own worrying mind is just as big of a problem to me. All too often I allow the worries and deceptions of the world to stifle the word that God wants to whisper in my ears and plant in my heart. (Matthew 13:22)

Silence can likewise be either sacred or evil. When it comes in the context of our cold-shoulders, our icy indifference to others, our fearful timidity in the face of injustice, or our lost and lonely self-inflicted prison cells, then silence can be profoundly evil.

But God is sometimes silent, and asks me to simply hear that silence and be content and at peace. In the titles of the first two sections, I have referenced the children of Israel (Psalm 95) and their grumbling at the Lord in the wilderness. They had seen God's mighty works and benefitted from his miraculous providence, and yet they grumbled and complained. As I reflected on my experiences in Bolivia, I felt convicted of such unrest. When I cried out to God to "do something!" about our misfortunes, He seemed to me to be responding by turning a deaf ear. I realize, now at least, how far that was from the truth.

God always answers our prayers. He knows our needs better than we do. His answers do not always follow our directives and timelines. In the Silence of Bolivia, God was being God, and that was enough. I am His beloved child and His providence is unfailing. I struggle to listen to this type of sacred silence and simply know that He is in charge. This Silence speaks of profound power and peace.

In the Silence of a prayer chapel I can, at times, sit and just be with Him for an hour, basking in awareness of Him; neither of us needing to "say" anything.

As Wilmer sat silently on Maria Luisa's lap, their love was evidence of a saintly being. They sang a silent song of such pure love, that even though this young boy never uttered a word, he lived a life that still touches the souls of my patients every day as they ask to hear his story. His silence is sacred.

A myriad of little consolations and "coincidences" have served to nudge me when I needed it. From tears to birds, to butterflies, to rainbows, breezes, shooting stars, songs on the radio... Squire Rushnell calls these "God winks" in his book *"When God Winks At You."* We should all learn to appreciate these more.

People. Oh, how He likes to speak to us through one another. Of course not everything people say can be taken as "heaven-sent", but every now and then the words of a spouse or a spiritual companion can hold within them some beautiful nuggets of Wisdom. Recognizing those can take some discernment, but when Michelle tells me "Maybe he is the one person we came up here to see" (Don Pedro), I best take heed. When Fr. Tom sends me out to make my first house calls in the hills of Arteaga, I can hear the invitation more clearly as Christ Himself asking me to go be His hands, His eyes, and His ears to minister to those suffering souls. (Saints and Influencers).

Lastly let me say a few words about The Word, Scripture. We have probably all had the experience of a word of scripture jumping out at us in some surprising or even miraculous way. Even scripture passages we've heard dozens of times before often take on new and poignant meaning when read in light of whatever situation we are currently facing.

When I read the Lord's Prayer a few years ago I received a little insight that was fresh and new to me. But I felt called to really study that insight and prayerfully "gnaw" on it for the next few months. My little reflection on The Authentic Lord's Prayer should only serve to challenge us to listen more intentionally and meditate more humbly as we listen to the deeper truths He wants to share with us.

I've said a few times in these stories "we hear more when we listen". Don't expect (or wait for) Him to knock you off your horse. Just start wherever you are and ask Him to talk to you, and practice being silent. Listening is not easy.

When you hear a profound Silence, rest in that. Don't try to force Him to fit your preconceived notions. He hears you. He loves you. Just listen to that.

God is being God; and that is always enough!

Stephen A Braden, M.D.

Dr. Stephen A Braden is available for book interviews and personal appearances. For more information contact:

Advantage Books
info@advbooks.com

To purchase additional copies of this book or other books published by Advantage Books visit our bookstore website at www.advbookstore.com

Longwood, Florida, USA
"we bring dreams to life"™